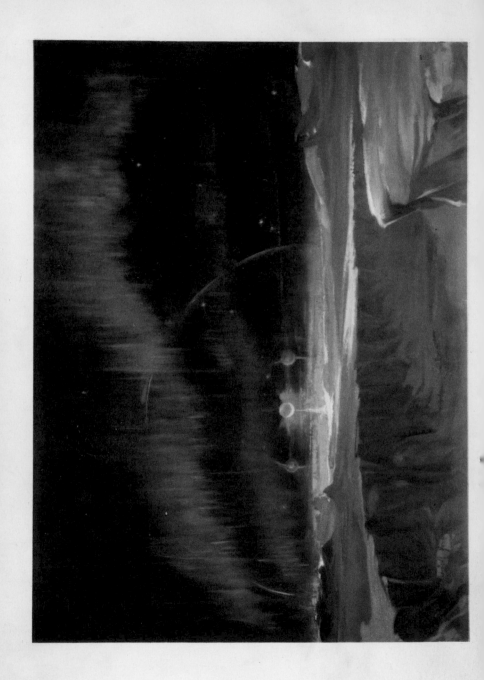

COLD

The Record of An Antarctic
Sledge Journey

BY

LAURENCE McKINLEY GOULD

Second in Command

BYRD ANTARCTIC EXPEDITION

With 47 illustrations from photographs by the author,
two maps and two color reproductions of paintings
by DAVID PAIGE

BREWER, WARREN & PUTNAM
NEW YORK 1931

To
M.R.G. AND G.P.P.

WHO HAVE DONE SO MUCH FOR ME
THAT I HAVE WRITTEN THIS BOOK
FOR THEM

CONTENTS

LIST OF ILLUSTRATIONS

vii

FOREWORD

BECAUSE in this most modern of expeditions, the dog sledge journey of the geological party was after the traditions of another day in polar exploration; because it enabled us to know the romance and the glamour of the days of Nansen and Peary and Shackleton and Scott; because it added much new information to our knowledge of the Antarctic, and perhaps most of all, because we had such great fun in doing it, I have wanted to tell the story of what has been generously referred to as the " last real polar sledge journey."

The story of the organization of the Byrd Antarctic Expedition and of its establishment at Little America on the Bay of Whales has been ably told in Admiral Byrd's " Little America." It was further Admiral Byrd's province, not mine, to give an account of the achievements and contributions of the various members of the expedition, and I have made no attempt to do that except in so far as they concern the story I am trying to tell.

Furthermore it is not possible for me to evaluate the work of the Byrd Expedition and to suggest its place in the roll of Antarctic expeditions. Not until the results of our scientific work are available will it be possible for anyone to do that and as senior scientist I am too close to the picture ever to do it. But against a history of expeditions, many of whose steps have been dogged with suffering and even death, it is no mean achievement just to have placed the largest expedition in the field that has ever wintered in the Antarctic and to have brought back every man without even a minor casualty. This in itself is perhaps the greatest compliment possible to the leadership of Admiral Byrd.

My story is concerned primarily with the sledge journey to the Queen Maud Mountains and the things that led up to it. Since these had their beginning in March 1929 with the loss of the Fokker plane in the Rockefeller Mountains, whither I had flown with Balchen and June to make a geological reconnaissance, my story opens with an account of our adventures on that enterprise. It carries on from there through the winter night of preparations and on throughout the sledge trek to our return to Little America in late January 1930.

Because words are such an inadequate medium for conveying impressions of color, and because David Paige has so aptly caught certain phases of Antarctic colors on his canvases, I am grateful for his friendly interest which has made possible the inclusion of reproductions of two of his paintings in this book. These are representative works from a series of nine oils which he made shortly after the return of the expedition to the United States. While he has not been in the Antarctic Paige has so steeped himself in the lore of it, that his work, to us who have been there, does have the charm of authenticity as well as unusual artistry.

In the background of preparation for my present interest in polar exploration and research, there has been the friendship of three men to whom I shall always be indebted. My teacher-friend, Professor Hobbs of the University of Michigan, with whom I had my first polar experience on the first University of Michigan Greenland Expedition, George Palmer Putnam under whose leadership and with whom I explored and mapped part of the west coast of Baffin Island, and Dr. Isaiah Bowman, Director of the American Geographical Society, whose friendly interest has from the beginning been a source of stimulation and inspiration. I want also to express my appreciation for the assistance I have so often had from O. M. Miller and W. L. Joerg of the American Geographical Society.

For me to tell of the specific contributions made by my companions of the expedition to the success of our sledge journey would entail a very lengthy story. Let me only say that the present book is the outgrowth of the understanding and friendship that came to me from the whole experience, and more particularly from the intimate contacts with my sledging companions.

LAURENCE McKINLEY GOULD

New York City,
June 10, 1931.

EXPLANATION

Since my interest in going to the Antarctic was to study whatever rocks and topography I could reach, I have not been able to escape occasional references to mountains and glaciers as geological and geographical features. But I have tried to avoid technicalities and I think there are but two words that need definition:

sastrugus (plural is sastrugi) — ridges of snow developed parallel or longitudinal to the wind direction. They may be formed by deposition or by wearing away of the surrounding snow. Ofttimes they consist of snow so tightly packed that it is scarcely less hard than ice. They are usually but a few inches in height but may in exceptional cases be as much as two or three feet high.

nunatak — an isolated hill or mountain surrounded by an ice sheet. They are usually thought of as typically marginal features of great continental ice sheets.

All distances in the text are given in statute miles, unless specifically indicated and all temperatures are in the Fahrenheit scale.

L. M. G.

It all began for me one day in March 1928 when I received a letter from Commander (now Rear Admiral) Byrd notifying me of my appointment to be geologist and geographer of his proposed Antarctic expedition. A busy summer of preparations and then on September 25th I shipped aboard the supply ship Eleanor Bolling from Norfolk. The other ship, the City of New York, had sailed from New York City exactly one month earlier, but being slower at sea, did not reach Dunedin, New Zealand, until a few days after the Bolling, near the end of November.

Followed days of feverish preparations and then our departure from Dunedin, our last port of call, on December 2nd with the City of New York in tow of the good ship Eleanor Bolling. This hastened our arrival at the north edge of the pack where the Bolling released the City and hurried back to Dunedin to bring down the two largest airplanes and the major part of our supplies.

The C. A. Larsen, a huge whaling ship, was about to begin its southward passage through the belt of pack ice and thanks to the good offices of her skipper, Captain Nilsen, the City of New York with most of the prospective winter party aboard was given a towline. Thus we found ourselves south of the pack in the open waters of the Ross Sea on December 23rd. On Christmas Day we sighted the northern edge of the Ross Shelf Ice or the Barrier and on the next day made our first landing at Discovery Inlet. We then sailed eastward along the face of this great barrier ice cliff to the Bay of Whales which we reached on the 28th.

Commander Byrd made a reconnaissance trip with dog

sledges to locate a site for our prospective permanent quarters. On January 1st, 1929 he returned to the ship and the active work of unloading began.

In the meantime he had appointed me as his second in command and now sent me inland to supervise the task of building Little America while he remained aboard ship to look after the hazardous work of unloading our supplies.

By the middle of January we had begun the erection of the first house in Little America and the one plane that we had brought along on the City of New York, the Fairchild, was unloaded and ready to fly. The first real aerial exploration was made by Commander Byrd, Balchen and June on the 27th when they flew east and north of Little America on a five hour flight; they discovered the Rockefeller Mountains. On this same day the Eleanor Bolling with its planes and supplies arrived and was unloaded with all possible speed so that she could return to New Zealand, with the hope of getting yet another load down to us. She headed back toward the north on February 2nd.

Except for three relatively short flights over territory eastward from Little America on February 18th no further exploration was attempted. All energy was concentrated upon the problem of moving our supplies inland to the village which was rising from the snow.

Ice conditions made it necessary for the Bolling to turn back from its projected voyage and on the 22nd of February the City of New York took its departure and thus insured our isolation at least until the following year.

Our living quarters were completed in the early days of March —— and here in the beginning of the twilight days that were to end the long summer light, begins the narrative called C O L D.

CHAPTER I

THE ROCKEFELLER MOUNTAINS AND A BLIZZARD

> " Black night,
> White snow,
> The wind, the wind!
> It will not let me go.
> The wind, the wind! "
> *From the Russian of* ALEXANDER BLOK.

WE awoke to a cool "milky" sort of morning on March 7th. It did not augur well for a good day to fly. Yet it seemed good enough for the dog teams to start south, on their projected trip for laying depots of supplies, preparatory to the more extensive establishment of such depots to be carried out in the spring before the polar flight.

Balchen and Braathen, each with a load of flags, departed immediately after breakfast to ski across the Bay of Whales and mark the trail to be followed by the dog teams. There was no little hurry and confusion getting the dog outfits ready. Four teams were to go. Norman Vaughan, Edward Goodale, Freddy Crockett and Jack Bursey were to drive their teams; Joe de Ganahl was to go along as navigator and Carl Peterson as radio operator. Vaughan was placed in charge of the party.

As the morning drew on the weather became markedly

better, and before noon Bill Haines, the meteorologist, assured me that we could not expect better weather at this time of the year. Now it was my turn to be in a hurry. Since their discovery by Commander Byrd on January 27th, I had been anxiously waiting for an opportunity to get over to the Rockefeller Mountains to make at least a preliminary survey before winter.

Hitherto the only known rock outcrops in King Edward VII Land had been the few nunataks of the Alexandra Mountains. Only one of these had ever actually been visited, and that by Prestrud [1] of Amundsen's South Polar Expedition in 1911. Nothing was known of their geology. The whole matter of the relationship of this part of Antarctica to the rest of the continent was a blank page. It seemed most desirable to make at least a brief survey here during our first season, for there would not be time for me to undertake studies both here and in the Queen Maud Mountains during our second summer.

Commander Byrd had not considered it practicable for me to attempt the trip until the ships were both under way for New Zealand, and so the season had become rather far advanced for flying before we could make the venture.

The entire matter of whom I should take and what I should take, on the proposed flight, was left in my hands. I decided on Bernt Balchen as pilot, and Harold June as co-pilot and radio operator. Upon their advice we decided to take the Fokker rather than the Fairchild, for the former would carry a more generous load of supplies.

We had been half ready for the flight for more than a week and were just waiting for the right weather. Even with Haines' assurance it didn't look too good to-day but

[1] Amundsen, Roald. *The South Pole*, vol. II, pp. 240–246.

Our Camp before the last Blizzard

The Ends of the Propeller Blades were curled
into Corkscrews

we were getting impatient. Most of our supplies had long since been loaded into the plane, and so it did not take Black long to check in the rest. By noon the plane was ready, but Balchen was out setting flags to guide the dog teams across the uncertain pressure ridges of the bay. Just about the time I was beginning to " chafe at the bit " he returned. He insisted that he was not the least bit tired from his strenuous ski trip and was accordingly all eagerness to take-off for the Rockefeller Mountains. It took him not more than five minutes to eat his lunch and an even shorter time to collect all the clothing and personal effects that he thought he would need on the trip.

Meanwhile it had taken the members of the sledging party all the morning to complete their preparations, and it so happened that both parties were ready to leave almost simultaneously. A flight was no new thing to us in Little America, but a sledging party starting out to lay bases was a new venture for any of us. Consequently we in the plane got little attention at the time of our take-off. To all appearances it was the most casual one that anyone had yet made. All hands, including our Rockefeller Mountain party, went down the hill that heads the little Ver Sur Mer Bay above which Little America was built, to bid the dog team party good-bye. Some of the boys followed along around the bend; a mere handful came back up the hill to see us off. I do not think it had really dawned on many beside Commander Byrd that whatever might happen to us, ours after all was bound to be an historic flight. It was to be the first flight ever made away from base over the Antarctic continent to make a landing and establish a temporary sub-base or camp.

We planned to land at the Rockefeller Mountains, establish our camp and keep the plane with us until we had completed our survey, and then fly back to Little America. After all we should be only about two hours flying distance from Little America, and so the whole thing seemed very simple. It turned out to be anything but that.

The field was very rough for a great many new sastrugi had developed during the blizzard which had just quieted down on the preceding day. We had become so used to having a good smooth field here that nobody thought it necessary to do any levelling off of the snow. What with our heavy load, it was a frightfully hard take-off. The skis banged against the hard ridges of snow until it seemed they would surely be smashed.

Finally we were in the air, and then instead of heading eastward at once, we turned southward to see if all went well with the sledging party. We flew low over them and they seemed to be getting on all right, so I radioed this news back to Commander Byrd. Balchen then nosed the Fokker eastward toward the Rockefeller Mountains. We flew for two hours before we saw the mountains and when we finally did sight them, we circled about to locate the most likely looking landing field.

To the south of the main group there appeared to be a great flat area where the landing would be easy, and from which the mountains would be easily accessible for our proposed topographic and geological surveys.

Not until we were near the ground did we sense the fact that the visibility had grown rather poor while we were in the air and that what had appeared a very flat surface was after all quite rugged. Balchen circled again. June dropped some smoke bombs so as to give him the wind direction on the ground. We then landed — rather roughly to be sure — but not nearly as roughly as I thought we would.

June immediately rigged up an aerial, using skis for masts, set up the radio, and soon assured those waiting for word back at Little America that we had landed safely and that all was well. Balchen and I secured the plane, put up the tent and made preparations for a hasty supper. It had grown late by the time supper was finished, so we decided to postpone any attempt to work until morning. Accordingly we all turned in for a good night's rest. Balchen should have been tired but he didn't seem to be. I have never seen his like nor do I ever expect to again. I came to know him under as difficult circumstances as one is apt to face. He never completely lost his poise. The word hardship seemed not to be in his vocabulary.

We were out early the next morning and were soon at work measuring a base line. There was a bit of breeze and the temperature was sufficiently low, so that one had to watch his fingers to keep from getting them frostbitten as he manipulated the theodolite. The breeze increased, and before noon there was so much drift that we could not take sights through it. It was getting too cold to attempt accurate work anyhow. But we had completed a sufficiently long base line to enable us to locate the main peaks within our sight.

We had a leisurely lunch inside our tent and were delighted to find that the wind was beginning to decrease. This was a good sign. We decided not to turn in. Time was so precious to us here that we had decided to work whenever the weather was good, whether it happened to be night or day, and then sleep during the bad weather.

Though we were beginning to get the first signs of the long night, yet we thought that when there were no clouds it would be light enough so we could do some surveying even at night.

By late afternoon the wind had dropped so much that there was little drift. There seemed no prospect of a sudden blow-up so we decided to visit at least the foot of the nearest mountain. We found the travelling frightfully hard as we neared the rocks for the surface was all ice. We had to go back and put on our ski boots and crampons; then a short climb and we were on the rocks — and what a disappointment! They were nothing but granite. Of course I had secretly hoped that I might find some sedimentary rocks, perhaps some fossils, and then the matter of correlating King Edward VII Land with other parts of the Antarctic would have been possible. But granite is a very awkward rock to use for establishing geological relationships in a land about which we know so little as we do about the Antarctic. But then I did not give up hope. Perhaps higher up or beyond we should later find some other sort of rock. It was too late and, what with overcast sky, too dark to attempt any farther climb at this time. We tramped back to our camp and turned in.

The Antarctic is a great place to sleep if one can keep warm. We all must have been sleeping soundly for not one of us had heard the wind which had been slowly mounting during the night. When I woke up at 6:30 and started to pull myself out of my sleeping bag, I found it was both snowing and blowing rather hard. Too hard, in fact, to attempt any work. I wriggled back down into my bag for another nap and advised Bernt and Harold to do likewise. By 11 o'clock I had had enough sleep and couldn't stand the bag any longer. Bernt and I got up, cooked some oatmeal and the three of us breakfasted — Harold luxuriously in " bed." It was evident that the wind had grown much stronger than it had been when I wakened at 6:30 but none of us thought it serious.

Suddenly one side of our tent collapsed; we thought the two tent guys that we had fastened to one of the skis of the plane had been torn apart by the force of the wind. Bernt looked outside.

" The plane has moved," he yelled. Our tent guys had been slackened by the short slide of the plane. Bernt and I scrambled out of the tent, to find a wind so strong that we found it difficult just to stand against it. We both sensed that the situation was serious and started shovelling snow onto the skis to help hold them down. The wind was growing stronger. The plane slid again. I jumped onto a ski to weight it down while Bernt frantically shovelled snow upon it. June was hurrying to join us. We needed his extra weight on the other ski. Whoever said that trouble was born twins was right. This had to be the one time that our primus stove leaked gasoline which caught fire in the bottom of the cooker. June had to put this out before he could join us.

We took turns with our one shovel cutting great blocks of snow which we piled high on the skis and in front of the fuselage. Balchen then made a dead man of skis and secured the landing gear to it with four strands of alpine rope. We decided to make a wall of blocks all along the front of the plane.

There came a lull in the wind about 2:30. In our ignorance of the capriciousness of Antarctic weather we thought this a sign that the worst was over. We had a breathing spell and made the tent guys fast again.

With complete suddenness and without any kind of warning the wind let go about an hour later with unprecedented violence. The plane moved again — slid back until the guys on the landing gear were taut, skidded around, quivered a bit and then was still. A sudden gust lifted the left wing, and it looked for a moment as if the plane would turn over. The wind was so strong that we could not stand upright against it but we scrambled over to the left wing on our hands and knees. It was impossible to get a line through the eye on the end of the wing. All three of us together could not brace ourselves against the force of the wind so as to reach it.

Another gust. The whole plane lifted and quivered. Only the dead man held it. We had to hold the left wing down somehow. I remembered that we had put a ball of heavy line in the grub box. I soon found it and, hanging to the free end, I threw the ball over the wing. I grabbed the two strands from either side of the wing and held on. Bernt soon had another line over. Meanwhile Harold was struggling with the shovel. June was the heaviest of the three of us. He would be of most value as an anchor so he relieved Bernt who redoubled his attempts to get a line through the eye on the end of the wing. I felt my hands getting numb and realizing that if it kept on I should, in spite of all my determination, let go the line. I was just able to reach a ski. I tied my lines around it and held on then with both my hands and legs.

Three times we were both lifted off the ground. Another feather and the plane would have overturned. We were getting colder all the time and still we dared not let go, for Bernt had not yet succeeded in getting a line on our end of the wing of the plane. He had, however, gotten one through the eye of the right wing and had that anchored to a dead man. I never saw a man work so like a madman as did Bernt.

The hard Antarctic snow scratched and stung like sand as it swirled about our faces. The angular crystals of the snow made the blizzard a veritable sand blast. My face grew numb as my beard became saturated with ice, and I had to blink vigorously to keep my eyelids from freezing shut. In my great haste to get out of the tent in the morning I had dressed hurriedly. I had put on short mits which left a gap between them and the sleeves of my windproof parka. My wrists soon lost all feeling. Hours later I found them both encircled with bracelets of blisters where they had frozen.

It was more than three hours before Harold or I dared move. By that time Bernt had finished with the right wing and had piled up enough snow blocks so that he could reach the end of our wing and secure a guy to it. We all turned to and piled snow blocks upon the dead man to which it was anchored. It was good to move about again though we did so now only with the greatest difficulty. We decided to anchor this wing further by securing the lines, that Harold and I had been holding, to other dead men. It did not seem possible that anything could move our plane now.

Still the wind blew with no indication of lessening. No one could stand erect. We leaned against it as one might against a brick wall. It seemed equally solid.

Handling the shovel to cut snow blocks was a real adventure. It possessed life. It would writhe and twist in

one's hands, and if the wind chanced to catch it broadside one had to let go or go tumbling head over heels.
We had to crawl to windward, then pick up a block of
snow and try to steer ourselves toward the place where
it was to be piled as the wind blew us back.

We quite lost account of time. We just worked. It
seemed days but it was only hours. We knew that if we
lost the plane it would cripple the planned aerial activities
of the expedition during the second summer. But of more
immediate concern was the realization that if we lost it
we might have to walk some 135 miles back to Little
America. This would not have been such an ominous prospect earlier in the season. But it was nearing the middle
of March, and we knew that the days would gradually
get colder and darker until the sun disappeared completely
sometime early in April. But we all realized that the possibility of losing the plane was imminent, so we unloaded
all of our supplies and the emergency radio outfit from it.

It was nearly midnight before we dared leave the ship
long enough to look to our tent. Two great holes had
been ripped in the one side when the guys were torn
loose. The tent floor was covered with soft wet snow. Our
sleeping bags and extra clothing were fairly saturated
with it. But the wind had dropped a bit, so we cleaned
things out as best we could and crawled into the soggy
bags. Fortunately the temperature was up to 25 degrees
above zero or we should have lain there and shivered or
frozen. We were quite dead tired and promptly fell asleep
in our Antarctic Turkish-bath sleeping bags.

It was not a long rest. Toward early morning the wind
was on the increase again. We were awakened by the din
of our tent cracking and snapping in the wind. It sounded

for all the world as if we were being bombarded with rifles. We could have scarcely felt less forlorn had such been the case.

Whether we could be of any use or not didn't matter. We had to get out and shovel snow. The plane quivered and shook with every strong gust of wind. But the guys and the dead men held, and with the afternoon the worst of the storm seemed to have passed. There was a bright sunset and then a few stars. I set up my theodolite about 10:30 to get some star sights. It was no use. The heavens were quickly overcast, so I crawled into the tent where Bernt and Harold were already asleep.

At 3:30 A.M. the frightful noise of our tent flapping in the wind awakened me. I had to get up for the plane was in danger. I dressed and went out to look things over. It didn't seem so bad outside as it had sounded inside the tent so I assured Bernt and Harold that everything was all right and went back to bed. But not to sleep. Three more times I became so uneasy that I got up to look at the plane. Finally I fell asleep not to waken until 10:30.

We all got out of our bags and shortly had two mugs of oatmeal apiece. The wind was quite mild now. It didn't seem to be blowing more than 25 to 40 miles an hour, but it was snowing heavily so there was no seeing anything. We only knew the plane was still with us when we got out and felt it.

At four o'clock Harold was successful in "raising" Little America. From time to time during the past few days he had sent messages to the effect that we were all right. Though we had not, during that time, been able to hear Little America they had heard June and had not been disturbed about us. We then learned that they had had no counterpart of our blizzard. The weather there was fit for landing. Though we had by no means completed the work we had hoped to do in the mountains, we had long since decided to fly back to Little America at the very first break in the weather. It seemed folly to tempt fate any further in the matter of keeping the plane. If the weather continued to improve it looked as though we might take off within a few hours. We arranged another radio schedule for 8 o'clock.

It was still snowing and the wind continued to blow though it appeared to be lessening. We were so anxious to believe that it would soon stop and that the weather would clear enough so that we might take off, that we made preparations to do so. We loaded a great many of our supplies and clothing back into the plane in preparation for our expected departure. But the wind did not calm down until 10:30, and then it was still overcast and so quite dark. But the temperature was falling and the barometer was fairly steady so we went to sleep optimistic about the morning.

The flapping tent woke me at 2:30. It seemed so bad that I dressed and went out and unloaded all of our foodstuffs and other supplies from the plane. And the barometer had begun to fall. Then suddenly the sky grew lighter and the wind decreased. Things looked so hopeful that I decided to wait up until 5 o'clock when it would be light enough for us to make plans to take off. But it was no use; shortly it began to snow so I went back to bed for an hour's nap before getting June out to keep his 7 A.M. radio schedule with Little America. His efforts were wasted for he was unable to raise the camp.

This was a gloomy day. Sometimes the wind sprang up

as though it were setting in for another blow. Then it would lull. But all the while the barometer continued to drop and the snow to fall. It was dead calm all the afternoon and soon the plane, the tent, in fact everything was covered with a blanket of soft snow five to seven inches thick.

That night of March 12th was the first quiet night we had had for some days. There was still a dead calm on the morning of the 13th, and it had stopped snowing but the sky was completely overcast. The visibility was impossible — there was no hope of flying. We decided to risk the weather and climb the mountains.

It turned out to be a most profitable day. We completed our triangulation and made a good collection of rocks. When we reached the top of the highest mountain near our camp we had our first comprehensive view of the whole group and it was disappointing. We found ourselves to be almost at the middle and on the southern side of a crescentic shaped group of scattered low-lying peaks and ridges almost completely covered with snow. Many of the smaller peaks and ridges appeared only as bulges beneath their heavy blankets of white. Only the higher more precipitous masses showed patches of bare rock, and the highest peak in the whole group measured but a little over 2000 feet above sea level.

In places the rocks had rounded surfaces and pockets, for all the world like those found in the desert developed by wind-sand erosion. Had we not been subjected to the " sand blast " of the snow in our recent blizzard, we might have been at a loss to explain these phenomena. I think they were developed by the abrasive action of the wind driven snow.

In sheltered places we found bits of gray lichens and in just one place some greenish moss-like growth. In this essentially lifeless continent any evidence of life is always of great interest.

We were greatly surprised to find that there is apparently a great deal of melting about the mountains during the warmer months. In many places thin layers of bluish ice flanked their upper slopes, and great fields of whitish snow-ice formed from the freezing of half melted snow stretched away from parts of the group as far as 7 to 10 miles. Near the mountains there were numerous scattered circular patches of darker ice which contrasted rather sharply with the general white or gray-white background. These ice fields looked as though they had a case of mammoth freckles. We learned that these " freckles " were caused by rocks which had rolled down from the mountain slopes and then melted themselves into the ice by heat absorbed from the sun during the warmer months of the year.

The snow-ice surface around the mountains is rarely more than 300 feet above sea level, and as one looked about him at the scattered peaks and ridges he could not help getting the impression that the aspect of the whole was more that of a group of islands in a sea of ice than a well defined group of mountains. It seems very likely that if the ice were to disappear they would in fact become an archipelago in a shallow sea.

It was a great disappointment to me, as we headed toward our camp, to realize that there was nothing in the character of the rocks or their structure that would enable me to correlate them definitely with other known lands in the Antarctic.

This had been the first and only real day of work in the field and we had finally completed the task we had flown over here to do. We could now hope for the opportunity to fly back to Little America without any feeling of guilt that we had failed to accomplish our projected task.

It looked as if the morning of the next day, March 14th, was to be the day. When I awoke at 5 o'clock there were but few clouds, and the whole aspect of things was so hopeful that I called Bernt and Harold and we began to get the plane ready to take off. While Bernt was placing the canvas cover over the motor and putting the torch below it to heat it up, and Harold was heating the oil over our cooker, I shovelled away at the snow wall that we had worked so hard to build up. But it was no use. We could not shut our eyes to the fact that it was slowly becoming overcast, and that soon the horizon would disappear in that curious chalky sort of day in which every direction looks the same and one can easily imagine himself suspended in a world of milk. On all sides an opaque white.

First there came little puffs of wind from the north. That was warning enough. We began all over again building our snow wall and further securing the plane, and kept at it all the morning. Perhaps it was quite as well that we were not able to take off for Harold was able to establish radio communication by the middle of the forenoon and we learned that the weather at Little America was unfit for flying. As a matter of fact there had not been a single day since we arrived in the Rockefeller Mountains favorable to a take-off and flight back to Little America — only 135 miles away. A short distance in a plane, but before we had covered it, it loomed very long to us.

About noon it let go again. Never was there another such blizzard. In one swoop the wind gathered up all the loose snow that had fallen during the period of calm. Great clouds of the icy flying dust swirled and flowed about us. The air became liquid. So completely saturated was it with snow that one could not face the wind and breathe. It was suffocating. We were utterly helpless. We could not even see our hands in front of our faces. Yet, strangely enough, even though the wind was on the increase the visibility gradually grew better. Within two or three hours, in spite of the ever increasing wind, the air was quite clear for all the loose snow had been blown away. All about us now was a hard half icy surface which the wind could not grip.

We were completely bewildered. We all knew that we were in a devil of a mess but we couldn't make ourselves stop to think about it. We had to keep busy. With infinite trouble we started cutting blocks of snow wherever we could find patches deep enough. Then we would try to put them on top of our snow wall. Often we would be caught broadside, tumbled head over heels and hurled 20 to 30 feet to leeward. Then we clawed our way back on hands and knees to try another block. Finally when we did get one in place on the wall we were trying to rebuild, we could lie back and watch it fade or melt away as it was eroded by the terrific force of the wind. We had never worked harder yet the wall always grew lower.

We had to stop at 3:30 for a breathing spell. We had a mug of hot cocoa and then tried to strengthen the wall about our tent before returning to the plane.

One time Bernt and I were trying to anchor an additional line to an end of the wing, when a sudden gust blew me off my feet and held me streamlined horizontally in the air for some seconds. And the wind was increasing all the time. Once I was knocked off my feet by a blow on the side of my head. Though he could not possibly have heard me, I started to tell Bernt what a clumsy ass he was with the shovel. I looked up to find that he wasn't within 40 feet of me. I just had time to dodge a piece of hard snow half as big as my head or I should have gotten another crack. It seemed that the whole earth was being torn apart. In spite of its hard glazed surface the wind was breaking loose great pieces of snow and sending them bounding along the ground or hurtling through the air.

Harold had tried intermittently all the afternoon to raise Little America but without success. But in every case he broadcast a brief account of the uncertainty of our position. Unfortunately none of these messages was picked up at Little America else they and those back in the States might later have been spared much worry. Because it was a better transmitter Harold always used the one in the plane. It was therefore necessary for him to be in the plane, when he was operating. Bernt and I got in with him at the 8:30 schedule. The wind, like all the big ones that had preceded it, was almost due north and the plane was headed directly into it. The force of the wind against the air speed indicator therefore gave some measure of its velocity. During the 8:30 schedule the registering needle hovered around 90 miles an hour.

Sometimes there would come lulls in which the air speed indicator would fall as low as 35 miles. We soon learned to dread these. They were always ominous. We held our breath, for we knew the wind would come on again fiercer than ever. With the terrific gust that always followed such lulls, the air speed indicator would run way over a hundred.

Though the motor was cold and very stiff, the force of the wind on the propeller was revolving it slowly. In spite of the five dead men holding it the plane quivered constantly as though it were ready to take off.

We tried to work at our wall again. But it was more than hopeless. Not only was it growing lower but the patch of snow upon which the plane and our tent were anchored was growing smaller.

When we landed and made fast the tent and plane on our arrival, we thought we had found an especially smooth flat area of shelf ice — which is really compacted snow. With the terrific winds, patches of blue ice began to appear. These grew ever larger. It appeared that we had stopped near the northern margin of what during the summer had been a snow-bound lake formed from the accumulation of thawwater from the mountain slopes. As the wind had continued to blow the areas of blue ice became blended into one, and this kept getting nearer and nearer to our camp. Now at 9 o'clock the snow had been all swept away to within 20 feet of the tail of the plane. It was evident that if the wind continued indefinitely, all the snow that was holding the plane and protecting our tent would be slowly eroded away and we should go with it.

The light was growing dim, and by 10:30 the wind had grown so strong that one could only crawl wherever he went. We could do no work and we were dead tired. The

HAROLD JUNE

BERNT BALCHEN
BOTH WERE TIRED OUT

THE RESCUE WITH WRECKED FOKKER IN BACKGROUND

possibility of the plane "taking off" any instant was so great that I refused to let Harold keep his radio schedule at 10:30. With our heads close together so that we could hear each other I yelled to my two companions that there was nothing we could possibly do now and that everything would be all right. They nodded in agreement. I think each of us knew that the other two were lying, but somehow it gave us a bit of comfort just to make the statement. Perhaps, though, neither of my companions gave up hope. It seems to me now, just two years later, that I don't think I ever really had any hope after the second onslaught of the wind.

We crawled into our cold wet tent and wriggled down into our still clammy sleeping bags. And there is nothing in all this world quite as clammy as a wet fur sleeping bag. It was some time before we slept. Outside the noise had been terrific. Inside it was deafening, for in addition to the constant howling and thundering of the wind itself was added the dreadful slapping and cracking of the tent. Not more than two feet of the peak of the tent projected above the snow wall about it, but this was enough for the wind to get a good go at it. I know full well that there may be a tendency for polar explorers in general to exaggerate at times just to get a right impression. But I do not know how to exaggerate about these things. I would never have dreamed — much less believed — that a little cloth tent could have been the instrument of such a din.

We went to sleep and it was not until 10:30 the next morning that we awoke. The noise still continued but was not so deafening and the sun was shining. I crawled out of my bag to see if everything was all right. I somehow knew that I would not see the plane. It is curious how inarticulate or prosaic one may sound in a tense moment such as this. I stuck my head out of the tent and pulled it back in with the almost laconic statement to Bernt and Harold — " The plane's gone." I think we had all sensed that it had been torn loose and blown away a few minutes after we had crawled into the tent the night before, but none of us dared suggest it to the others. Certainly it was no surprise to any of us to find it gone now. One's mind works in a funny way at such times.

I had not thought to take a look to see whether or not the plane had been blown so far away that we couldn't see it. I looked again. There it was from a half to three quarters of a mile away across the blue ice to the leeward. It looked intact. It was sitting upright on its skis and the wings appeared whole. I imparted the news to my two aviator companions that after all the plane was unharmed, that it had just skidded across the ice. They smiled but said nothing.

The wind was still far too strong to attempt to stand, but nothing would do but that Bernt must go over and see what had happened to the plane. He dressed and pulled himself out of the tent. We watched as the wind sent him slithering across the ice. Presently he started back. We could see him coming but he seemed to get no nearer. He had to crawl most of the way back on his hands and knees.

Perhaps June was not surprised by the report which Balchen brought back, but I certainly was. I had been in dead earnest when I first looked across the ice at the plane and reported to my companions that it appeared to be intact. I thought at the time that it would fly again, but it appeared from Bernt's account that it was a total wreck.

Only the wing was fairly sound. The fuselage and skis had been completely smashed.

We stirred about and had some breakfast, and then Harold tried to rig up the emergency radio set. A rather grim surprise awaited us here; the set was dead; the tubes were all out of commission. Our only hope now was that the crash of the plane had not wrecked the regular transmitter. It was silly to attempt to investigate until the wind calmed down somewhat. It blew all day, and we had to sit still and contemplate the fairly dismal prospect ahead of us.

I was perhaps more deeply disturbed over the matter of the sheer loss of the plane than the others. Of course we all realized that it would be a serious blow to the projected aerial activities of the expedition during the second season, but it was further a great misfortune that this first landing away from base in the Antarctic should have ended so tragically. That was a bad precedent. It was probably my insistence on the importance of getting to the new mountains this first season that brought about the trip. The loss of the plane was more surely my fault than any one else's. But it was gone, and as I review the precautions we took to save it I can think of nothing else that we could have done. In our ignorance of Antarctic winds, though we were all familiar with Mawson's records [2] in Adelie Land, we had unconsciously fallen into the habit of interpreting weather and winds in terms of what we had experienced in Little America. I think even had it been anchored with steel cables it would have been blown to bits where it stood. The only thing that might conceivably have saved it would have been to raise the tail. Bernt and Harold

[2] Mawson, Douglas. *The Home of the Blizzard*, Lippincott, vol. 1, pp. 112–116. Recorded wind velocities over 100 miles per hour.

knew this but there was no possible way to do it. We found that snow blocks would not hold it up.

To be sure our thoughts and regrets at the loss of the plane were somewhat overshadowed by a realization of the uncertainty of our own position. We had expected to be gone from Little America but a few days. We had brought a good month's supply of food with us and had an abundance of fuel in the gas tanks of the plane, provided they were still intact. But if we were forced to attempt to walk back to Little America at this late time of the year it might take us at least a month, for our experience had taught us that we could not depend on favorable weather for even half the time. I think Bernt could have done this trek with comparative ease. He is the ablest man out of doors that I have ever seen. But Harold and I were quite inexperienced on skis, and the long trek pulling a sledge load of supplies might have been too great for us. And of course before we had reached Little America the sun might have disappeared for its long winter sojourn, with the increasingly lowering temperatures that this would mean.

We spent the whole day more or less aimlessly discussing plans as to how we could, unassisted, get ourselves out of this predicament. The necessity for this did not seem particularly imminent, for we all thought that as soon as the wind calmed enough we could go over to the plane and Harold could start the radio and tell Commander Byrd of our plight. With the first good weather the Fairchild could fly over to get us. It seemed quite simple. And with sanguine feelings we went to sleep.

The positive knowledge that we could no longer count on the plane and that it was definitely disposed of was after all a relief, and we slept as we had not done for many days. Saturday morning we awoke to find the weather quite calm but not clear. We dressed and breakfasted and then went over to inspect the wreck and to try to establish communication with Little America.

In its pitifully broken condition the Fokker seemed even more possessed of a personality than it had before. The fuselage was torn and twisted, the skis smashed and splintered and the ends of the propeller blades were curled into corkscrews. The force of the wind had been so great that it had been spinning the propeller and thus turning over the motor at a great rate else this could not have happened. Only the wings were practically intact. They had been broken a little at the ends where the guy lines had been torn loose. It appeared that the plane had preserved its equilibrium in the air and had literally flown itself, tail foremost, for more than half a mile before it crashed onto the ice. We judged that the wind which caused all this must have blown at least 150 miles an hour.

June got out the emergency motor generator and tried the radio. He worked at it all day but without being able to raise Little America; no more was he able to hear any messages from there. I wandered back to our tent in the late afternoon to get the evening hoosh. From time to time I could hear the hum of the generator as Harold renewed his efforts with the radio. No one could have been more devoted to the problem ahead of him than Harold, and I am sure no one could have handled the emergency outfit more intelligently.

And then the crank shaft of the power outfit broke. It could not be fixed, and there was now no hope of telling our troubles to Commander Byrd. June had, however, been able to hear the camp at last. They had heard none of our messages just before the loss of the plane. They did not know of our second blizzard and so did not suspect our plight. They planned to broadcast to us hourly and expected us to fly back the next morning!

We were startled this day to have three skua gulls light near our camp. They were the first living things we had seen and should have cheered us. Perhaps they did. But somehow I could not keep myself from thinking of them as the vultures, the scavengers of the Antarctic!

Even though the day had been calm the weather was still ominous for it was too warm. The temperature was way up to 29 degrees above zero. Throughout all our bad weather and big winds the temperature had rarely gotten down to zero. Just one night it went to 11 below but then there was little wind. For the most part it ranged from 14 to 20 degrees above zero. Here was an application of the proverbial truth that " The Lord tempers the wind to the shorn lamb," for it is literally true that we could not have lived in such winds as we had endured had the temperature been low. In the course of our stay in the Antarctic we learned that high winds were always accompanied by rising temperatures. In one blizzard the temperature rose 65 degrees in 24 hours.

Saint Patrick's Day was the first good day we had had since our arrival! It was really the very first time that we could have safely taken off to fly back " home." We were up fairly early and Harold began his vigil with the radio receiver. Our long continued silence had caused Commander Byrd and the others to become genuinely alarmed. He told us again that the weather there was all right for our return, but in the meantime indicated that they were making preparations to come to look for us. A sledging party was being equipped to start for us and the Fairchild would fly as soon as possible.

I think Commander Byrd's most outstanding characteristic is his concern for the safety of his men, and so I realized something of his thoughts. The whole matter of coming to our rescue and of preparing people in the States for a possible catastrophe could not have been handled more intelligently. Naturally our failure to make contact with Little America over a period of three days had disturbed everyone. It was the most natural thing in the world to fear that we had crashed on a take-off, had fallen into a crevasse, had been buried beneath an avalanche or that something equally dire had happened to us. Curiously enough, the very thing that *had* happened to us had not occurred to anyone as a possibility.

But it was a hard pill for us to swallow — to have to sit by and hear this disturbing news being sent back to the States and not be able to reassure everyone of our well being; for we knew what concern such news would make in many quarters.

Not even Saint Patrick's Day could be good throughout its length. The sky became overcast in the afternoon, and it began to snow. All this made it increasingly apparent to us that there might come no time when it would be possible for the Fairchild to fly to our rescue. We therefore continued our plans for a possible walk back. We had food enough to make the journey if we used it sparingly, but the fuel was a serious matter. The crash of our plane had so wrecked its gas tanks that there were none which we could use for storage. Harold emptied the contents of the fire extinguishers that were in the plane and we filled these with gas. But this would not be enough to take us back. I decided to try dry cooking some food, particularly oatmeal, so that we could use it without consuming precious fuel to cook it on the trail.

The bad weather was short lived. March 18th was bright and sunny. We bolted our breakfast and sat breathlessly by as Harold slipped the receivers over his ears. Shortly he shook his head. The weather was still bad in Little America, and it was impossible for the plane to take off.

In the middle of the morning Harold listened again only to hear that the weather was still unsettled and for the third day to be informed that the dog teams would leave that day! ! ! Only one who has tried to equip a dog sledging party for fall travel can realize the myriad details that must be attended to before it can start, but we were abnormally impatient. It was so hard just to sit and wait. I think we should have been happier trudging along pulling on our hand sledges, but we all knew that our chances of being found, if we started out, would be very remote; whereas our present position was known to Commander Byrd, and both the plane party and the dog teams would know where to look for us. There was nothing to do but wait.

The weather did improve at Little America, and when Harold listened in at the 4 o'clock schedule he heard the plane in the air. We laid out a " T " of orange flags at the best place for landing we could find, then we got ready to set off some smoke bombs in case they did not see us at once from the plane.

We heard the plane long before we could see it for there were many clouds and the visibility was bad. Straining our eyes in the direction of the sound we at last saw it high up and flying almost over us. We set off smoke bombs and we yelled and waved our arms — not that this availed anything but to relieve us. The plane circled back. They had seen us.

There was a good deal of relief on all sides. Hanson as radio operator and Dean Smith as pilot were in the plane along with Commander Byrd. Smith did a superb job. I don't think it could have been done better. It was dusk when he landed and the field was rough but he set the plane down smoothly.

It was growing late and there was no time to lose. It was impossible for all six of us to return in the plane. Commander Byrd sent Balchen and June back with Smith, and he and Hanson remained with me. We expected them back for us the next morning.

The Commander had planned to have the plane make two more trips so that our most valuable supplies and equipment could be brought back to Little America. But the 19th, the 20th and the 21st passed without the weather being good enough for Smith to take off at Little America to return for us. Again the prospect of walking home loomed before us. We went about making preparations for such an emergency. The Commander hoisted a sail for the sledge hoping that if we attempted to walk the wind might help us a bit.

Meantime with new equipment Hanson had kept good radio communication with the base, and so we knew that on the 19th the dog teams had started for us. But we did not have to wait for them. At 6:30 in the morning of the 22nd we were told that the Fairchild was about to take off to come for us. All plans for making two flights were of course called off. We had to leave almost all of our gear in our mountain camp. We brought food in case we should have a forced landing on the way home and a few of my rocks. I even had to leave my rock hammers.

Smith was at the controls again and with him was June as radio operator. The five of us made a heavy load in the plane but with his usual ease Dean took off and we were soon headed westward. We passed over the sledge party that was bound for us, and within an hour and a half we were landing at Little America.

There was much handshaking and thumping on the back and friendly chaffing about the party that was " lost in the mountains." Throughout the winter we stoutly maintained that we had never been lost, that we knew where we were all the time, and that a man is not lost if he knows where he is. We were but "marooned." But there was no living down our reputation. Just when we thought everybody had forgotten about it, we would hear a message from the States on a Saturday afternoon broadcast, expressing relief that the party that had been " lost in the mountains " had been rescued. Then one day Joe Rucker suggested that the initials in my name, L.M.G., must surely stand for " Lost in Mountains Gould."

CHAPTER II

THE WINTER NIGHT

Deep and still
Is the winter night.
The silence is a garment of peace
That fits one closely.

JEAN RICE

for the night
Hath been to me a more familiar face
Than that of man; and in her starry shade
Of dim and solitary loveliness,
I learned the language of another world.

BYRON

ALL things are relative. Little America seemed the acme
of luxury after the discomforts and uncertainty of the
Rockefeller Mountains. I think it must have been some
days before I fell into the " swing " of things again.

I learned that the sledging party which had started south
the day we took off on our ill-fated flight had also been
somewhat unfortunate in their weather, though they had
known nothing comparable with a Rockefeller Mountain
blizzard. Much of the time it had been too bad for them
to travel, and after they had reached a distance of 46 miles
south of Little America they had been ordered back by
Commander Byrd. They had left caches of food and fuel
at distances of 20 miles, 41 miles, and 46 miles respectively

south of Little America, along the trail which they had carefully marked with flags at half mile intervals.

This experience was just what they needed to prepare them for what must certainly have been a much more serious venture had it been necessary for them to carry it out, namely to come all the way to the Rockefeller Mountains to search for us. As soon as Commander Byrd began to get disturbed about our safety he set the dog drivers to work preparing for such an emergency. Greater care was needed in making these preparations than had been necessary for the brief southward depot laying trip. It meant sledging under increasingly cold conditions with the daylight hours decreasing perceptibly each day, and finally with considerable uncertainty as to the length of time the journey might consume.

They had completed their careful preparations and left Little America on the 19th of March, headed toward the Rockefeller Mountains with supplies for a three months' journey. The teams were divided into two groups — an advance party in charge of Norman Vaughan consisting of four teams driven by Vaughan, Goodale, Bursey, and Thorne, with Peterson as radio operator and Joe de Ganahl as navigator, and a supporting party in charge of Arthur Walden consisting of three teams driven by Walden, Braathen, and Siple.

The supporting party turned back at 46 miles east of Little America while the advance party carried on until they had covered 63 miles where they were camped, when we flew over them on our way back to Little America from the Rockefeller Mountains.

So soon as the advance party knew that we were safe, they turned about and headed back toward Little America and made the entire distance back without a stop for camp and with the thermometer wavering between 30 and 40 degrees below zero — an extraordinarily good day's run when one considers that sledging at such low temperatures is strenuous work for the dogs.

With the return of this sledging party which had set forth to rescue us, all of the proposed field work for our first season was ended. All of our attention was then actively turned to the task of getting Little America ready for the long dark ahead.

In the course of the next three weeks we became transformed from a community which, during the summer months, had been able to pursue its work actively in the open or on the surface to one that lived and worked beneath the " ground."

There were a few supplies still to be hauled in from our so-called " barrier cache." This was a temporary dumping depot which we had established about 5 miles north of Little America near the edge of the shelf ice, to expedite the unloading of the Eleanor Bolling, so that she could start back toward New Zealand with the prospect of bringing a second load of supplies down to us. Most of the work of digging out the things in this cache and bringing them in to Little America had been accomplished under Captain McKinley's direction during my absence in the Rockefeller Mountains. I was back in time to take part in only one day's work at this task. That was quite enough. It was bitter cold and thoroughly unpleasant work, prospecting about in the snow with shovels and crowbars looking for things that might have escaped discovery.

Bernt and his aviation gang dug holes in the shelf ice for the Ford and Fairchild planes and then built hangars

of snow blocks around them. The commissary supplies,
which had not been used as walls for the big tunnel connecting our two main houses, were housed inside in a large
snow supply room which was built off the main tunnel
but connected with it. Dr. Coman followed this example
and had a similar room built to house his medical supplies.
Hanson and his radio assistants had gotten their equipment
inside by combining a snow house with the crate that had
held the fusilage of the Fairchild. The non-magnetic house
that had been especially designed and built back in the
States to house Frank T. Davies' various magnetic instruments had been left in New Zealand. A less enthusiastic
scientist might have thrown up his hands in despair —
but not " Taffy." Principally with the help of Chips
Gould, the carpenter, he succeeded in getting two snow
houses built in which he carried out his observations
throughout the winter, under the most adverse conditions
imaginable.

Captain McKinley looked forward toward the winter
night as a time for completing the developing and print-
ing of the aerial photographs he had taken during the
summer. His also was the task of cataloging and caring for
all the photographic work of the expedition aside from the
motion pictures. Such work necessitated a dark-room. Of
all the various structures in Little America none seemed to
have developed more magically than this. We thought all
the possible building materials had long since been used
up, but from somewhere Chips found enough to build a
double roomed dark-room which was adequate for the
photographic work.

Czegka had gotten all of his drills and lathes and other
tools indoors and finally succeeded in getting them

mounted between the mess hall and the Norwegian House — a space which he had to share with the power plant but which came to be known as the machine shop.

The matter of taking care of the dogs for the winter had given us a good deal of thought, and finally, after much discussion, it was decided that the best arrangement would be to house them in some sort of tunnels where they could be fed and taken care of in any kind of weather. Accordingly tunnels about three feet wide were cut into the snow, and the individual wooden crates, in which the dogs had lived above the ground, were put into the walls so that the front of the crate was just flush with the wall of the tunnel. The crates were spaced sufficiently far apart so that the dogs, which were attached to the fronts of them with short lengths of chain, could easily get in and out and have a bit of exercise but could not quite reach their neighbors. The tunnels were then roofed over. Except for Walden's and Braathen's teams these tunnels were arranged according to teams and so connected that all were accessible to a great central snow house which came to be known as the "chopping house," for here the seal meat was sawed and cut into pieces for the individual dogs.

Walden and Braathen had been collecting odd bits of lumber all summer which they planned to combine with an airplane engine crate in the building of a separate house in which to live. Chris Braathen is nothing if not resourceful and the house that resulted excited the envy of us all. In order to have their teams near them where they could more easily be taken care of, these men built tunnels for their dogs adjacent to this house rather than with the other dog teams.

The administration building or the Edgar Barratt House

and the mess hall or the Roswell Barratt House were heated by coal; the Norwegian House or Biltmore and the darkroom were heated by kerosene stoves. In the mess hall the coal had to do the double duty of cooking all of our food and heating the building. Coal was one of our most precious supplies, and we did not have enough to warrant the issuing of a regular amount to Walden and Braathen to heat their own little house. They had anticipated this, and Braathen designed and built a very efficient stove from a gasoline drum in which they planned to burn seal blubber for fuel. It is true that seal blubber is an efficient fuel — it does give off a great deal of heat, but in so doing it also liberates one of the most persistent and not altogether pleasant odors that I know of, with the result that Walden and Braathen led a much more exclusive life than they had ever expected to. In spite of all attempts to give this dwelling a more poetic name it was always referred to as " Blubberheim."

By the very nature of their work Haines and Harrison, the meteorologists, could not plan to carry on all of their activities under cover even in the winter time. They did, however, contrive to build a kind of snow house adjacent to the Administration Building from which they could send up their balloons throughout the winter without getting entirely out of doors. Indeed Bill Haines arranged the recording end of things so that he could stay well inside the house within the warmth of the stove while Harrison watched the balloon from the snow observatory just outside. In justice to Bill I must say that he occasionally went outside and did his work too.

By the end of the second week in April most of these things had been attended to, and, without sensing it, we

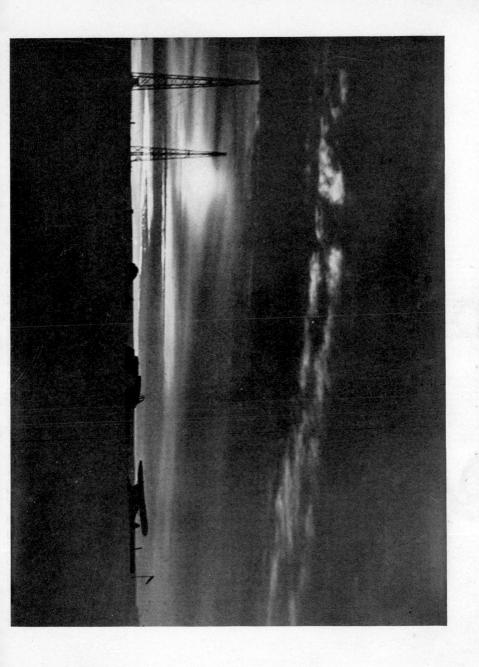

THEODOLITE COVERED WITH FEATHERY CRYSTALS OF
FROST OR RIME

had almost entirely taken on our ground-hog like existence for the winter. The last days of March and the first
few in April seemed more normal in that they gave us
alternating periods of daylight and darkness, but they were
generally cold. The thermometer seemed always to be
hovering around 40 degrees below zero or lower. At such
temperatures we found it difficult and even unsafe to
work hard out of doors for periods of more than two or
three hours at a time.

Each day the sun got perceptibly lower and the periods
of daylight very noticeably shorter. But this was withal
the most gorgeously colorful time of all the year. The snow
had lost its chalky or marble whiteness of the summer
when the sun was high. Now it was shimmering with colors that one could never exactly identify as blue, purple,
opalescent, or rose. And more than once in the latter days
of March, I was stopped in my tracks by the glory of the
setting sun. Most often were to be seen rich reds and royal
purples widely fringing the ragged stratus and cumulo-
stratus clouds that hovered about the horizon. If there
were no clouds then the sun became a flame scarlet ball,
sometimes surrounded with the most complicated and
fantastic halos and mock suns.

Not infrequently the air was filled with minute frost
particles which caught the light and color from the sun
and diffused it throughout the surrounding atmosphere.
The whole world became saturated with color. The sunset was not a thing far away — one participated in it. One
had a very real illusion of being suspended in a world of
soft pastel colors. One evening Russell Owen and I were
walking toward the mess hall about supper time with a
sunset directly ahead of us. We were with all seriousness

discussing the matter of just how far away it began, and neither of us placed it at more than 20 yards.

During the dark stretches of this colorful twilight, that was ending our all day summer, we began to get our first glimpses of the aurora australis or the " southern lights." With the coming of full darkness we had more spectacular displays, yet I shall not forget my first sight of one on a night early in April; a shaft of greenish white light streaming up from the horizon to the east that soon arched the heavens in a dancing band of light. Suddenly it was faintly aflame with all the hues of the spectrum. It was a rainbow which seemed to be infused with the spirit of jazz.

Though the sun did not disappear below the horizon until the 19th of April, we began our winter schedule on Monday the 12th. Breakfast from 8:30 to 9:30 and dinner or supper at 4 in the afternoon. For those who wanted a midday " snack " there was an Antarctic buffet luncheon ready at 1 o'clock.

And so the long night began. On a continent as large as the United States and Mexico combined we were the sole inhabitants. Little America was built on the northern fringe of a great floating shelf of ice more than a quarter of a million square miles in area. There were 1600 feet of water beneath us and the nearest land that had ever been seen was 135 miles away. More complete geographic isolation than ours could scarcely be imagined; but it was a group isolation. Individual isolation was about the most unattainable thing in Little America. There were 42 of us living in very compact quarters — much more intimate than had any of us ever lived before for any such period of time. Only Commander Byrd had a private room — the rest of the living quarters of our community were more or less common property. For any of us to have attained the privacy of the proverbial goldfish would have been a luxury that we did not even dream of.

A more cosmopolitan group in every sense of the word than ours had perhaps never been brought together for a polar night. There were 5 men from Norway, 1 from Greece, 1 from Czechoslovakia, 1 from Newfoundland, 1 from Wales; and from the United States — 5 from New York, 5 from Massachusetts, 3 from Washington, D. C., 2 from Pennsylvania, 2 from Connecticut, 2 from Missouri, 2 from Michigan, 2 from California, 2 from Washington State, 1 from Virginia, 1 from Minnesota, 1 from Ohio, 1 from Mississippi, 1 from Illinois, 1 from New Jersey, 1 from Florida, and 1 from New Hampshire.

In addition to the pilots, aviation mechanics, and such scientists as one would expect to make up such an expedition as ours, we had a boy scout, a circus acrobat, a sealing captain, a carpenter, a marine engineer, an amateur pugilist, a forester, a tree surgeon, an ice cream manufacturer, and a journalist! There was one trade or profession which was, however, absent, but the possible inclusion of which had furnished me some amusement. It happened that shortly after Commander Byrd had announced my appointment as geologist and geographer of the expedition, in the early spring of 1928, I was seated in my office at the University of Michigan when a young man walked in. He seemed very intense and earnest.

" Professor Gould," he said, " I want to go on this Byrd Expedition. I'll do anything under the sun to go, and you have no idea how hard I can work. Will you please use your influence with Commander Byrd to help me to get on the expedition? "

" I don't think I have any particular influence with the Commander," I replied. " You may write to him if you wish, but unless you are somewhat of a specialist, unless you can do some specific and necessary task better than anyone else who applies your effort will be wasted. What is your trade or profession? "

" I am an undertaker! " he replied.

Why were they here? Why did they all want to come? What interest could a forester, for instance, have in the Antarctic? Some came for sheer love of adventure and wanted no reward beyond that; some wanted fame or its counterfeit, publicity; some were mercenary and thought primarily in terms of what they were going to get out of it; and lastly there was that small group, the like of which gives character to any expedition of merit — not necessarily scientists at all, but men who could understand the lure, if not the love, of knowledge for its own sake; men who came not for position or money but who found full reward for their effort, in the pursuit of an ideal.

We represented a veritable museum of religious faiths. There were Greek and Roman Catholics and almost as many protestant faiths as there were persons. It would have been manifestly impossible to have devised any form of service that would have given even partial expression to so much variety of religious thought. We thought it better not to attempt it, and I have never been among a group of men, anywhere under any circumstances, where there was more complete religious tolerance than there was among us.

As the daylight hours had lessened so also had the necessity for work out of doors, with the result that we passed into the winter phase of our existence without any notice-

able break. In the construction of Little America it had
been my duty to look after the necessary working details,
now as executive officer it was still part of my job to see
that details were arranged to take care of the work of
running the camp. I have never believed in the volunteer
system among any such group of men; it would have meant
that a large part of the work would have been shouldered
by a few men. Accordingly every man had to take his turn
at washing dishes, hauling in coal, shovelling snow into the
snow melter, or whatever the task might be. In addition
we decided to have a man on watch throughout the whole
time. This meant a " night " watchman.

This was important from the standpoint of making regular meteorological observations and for keeping a record of
auroral displays. At first this detail, like all the rest about
camp, was filled by each man taking a turn at it, but early
in the winter Pete Demas volunteered to assume the task
for the whole dark time so that he could have some quiet
hours for study. He had early learned how difficult it was
to find peace and quiet during the waking hours of the
other 41 men in Little America. Anyhow everyone was
glad to let Pete take the job.

There were some members of our winter party who had
to contemplate the winter ahead, not as a time for more
respite from their work, but, as a necessity for accomplishing it under increasingly difficult conditions. Haines and
Harrison had to carry out their meteorological observations regardless of weather conditions; Davies had to keep
an almost constant watch over his recording instruments
out in their snow houses. Keeping the clockwork of such
mechanisms running regularly when the temperature fell
down to 40, 50, and 60 degrees below zero was an accom-

plishment in itself. But Taffy Davies and the two meteorologists were surprisingly successful at it.

Malcolm Hanson not only planned to carry on extensive experimentation indoors in his improvised laboratory, but he hoped to make out-of-door measurements from
time to time throughout the winter. He did this work in
spite of great odds. I don't think anyone worked more
unceasingly to accomplish the projects he set out to do
than did Hanson. He was ably assisted by Mason and
Peterson.

And there was George Tennant, the cook — certainly
his work did not get any lighter with the coming of winter.
It would have been difficult to have found anyone anywhere who would have done as much work as George did
and have done it with such good humor. Fortunately for
him Arnold Clark wanted to get some practice in cooking
and volunteered for the job of second cook. Arnold not
only acquitted himself well at this task but he also became
Taffy Davies' chief assistant in his magnetic work.

For the rest of us the winter night loomed as an opportunity for relief from regular or systematic work. But it
was not a time of idleness — our first field season had
hardly passed before we were beginning to make plans
and preparations for the second. Before the end of April
Commander Byrd was making assignments to various tasks
for this very work and it was at this time that my own plans
for getting into the Queen Maud Mountains became associated with the projected base-laying work of the dog
teams.

With the loss of the Fokker in the Rockefeller Mountains, it became evident that I could not expect transporta-
tion by plane for my planned geological work in the Queen

Maud Mountains. But if I were to get far enough into these mountains to do any real work by dog teams, it would mean a much more extensive program of sledging than had been anticipated just to lay bases for the polar flight. To make this possible it was decided to have the main sledging party, of which I should be a member, reinforced by a supporting party. Our preparations began with the designation of these two parties by Commander Byrd. They were first called the supporting party and the southern sledging party; the name of the latter was shortly changed to the geological party. The supporting party was to be composed of Arthur Walden as leader assisted by Chris Braathen, Joe de Ganahl, and Jack Bursey. The geological party was to be composed of Norman Vaughan, Freddy Crockett, Edward Goodale, John S. O'Brien, George (Mike) Thorne, and myself as leader.

It was at once evident that in just carrying out the work of getting ready for the sledging journeys we should have to draw upon nearly all of the resources of the camp. Accordingly committees were appointed by Commander Byrd to assist with the preparations. These committees included so many of the men in camp beside the sledging parties that the sledge journey became a project in which everyone felt a proprietary interest.

As we settled down to the routine of our work and play for the dark months, it became quite general practice to use the hours between breakfast and supper for whatever details or special tasks had to be accomplished. With supper so early we had a long "evening." Except for the hours when the "University of Antarcticâ" was in session, this time was largely given over to various forms of recreation.

There had been so many requests for some systematic instruction that we created the "University" which opened on May 6th with a course in geology, which consisted of two lectures and two discussion groups of an hour each per week. Shortly afterward Hanson began a series of lessons devoted to the theory and practice of radio operation and reception. This was a most important course, for from its training came Joe de Ganahl who was radio operator for the supporting party and Freddy Crockett, radio operator for the geological party. Many others developed sufficient skill to have handled radio sets for emergency purposes. To complete the curriculum of the "University" Harold June gave a series of lectures in aeronautics.

It seemed that almost everyone at some time or other during the day indulged in some sort of game. Bridge was early established as the most highbrow game. Most of us played at it only spasmodically. There was but one foursome consisting of Commander Byrd, Joe Rucker, Harry Harrison, and Captain McKinley which played together consistently throughout the winter. The rest of us were more apt to be found during the long evening hours indulging in the lowly games of poker or hearts with cigarettes or chocolate as stakes. We had no money nor would it have been of any use. Our bartering was done in terms of these two precious commodities. With the passing of the days the old navy game of Acy Ducy, which has been taken into the parlor, as it were, and called backgammon, became extremely popular. In fact I think that by the end of the winter it was more widely played than any other game.

There were just three recognized winter pastimes in which all the camp could join: radio broadcasts, Sunday

night movies, and our local talent shows. It is almost needless to state that our weekly broadcasts were one of the
most important sources of interest and recreation. They set
Saturday off from the rest of the week, and for this reason
alone served to break up the too close continuity of our
days. Unfortunately our reception of the musical portions
of the programs was rarely very satisfactory, but the spoken
voices were usually quite good.

We were always just a little bit on tenterhooks during
these broadcasts for fear that we would receive no messages
or that if we did they might be of an embarrassingly personal nature — for we remembered that these broadcasts
were not only directed to us by special short waves but were
also simultaneously broadcast by standard wave lengths
and anyone back home who wished could hear them. As
the winter passed we became mildly interested or absorbed
in each other's domestic or personal affairs as they were
revealed by messages we used to hear. One man in particular seemed almost equally popular with two girls who
rarely missed a weekly broadcast to remind him of their
affection. In the best of good humor we used to " razz "
him about it and bet on who would be the winner. Since
returning to the States this man has become engaged, but
whether to Edwina or Arlene I don't know.

Our moving pictures were reserved for Sunday nights.
Whoever selected these pictures for us must have realized
that men who are segregated as we were for the polar
night, are bound to be socially and sexually deprived. It
appeared that they had been almost too obviously selected
to avoid themes that could by any flight of fancy lead one's
mind into such channels. We were amused — very greatly
— by this fact. But we had a few very good productions

such as Chang, Grass, Nanook of the North, and some of
Charlie Chaplin's earliest comedies.

Our community entertainment reached its greatest
heights in the occasional home talent attempts. That for
the Fourth of July surpassed and eclipsed all subsequent
efforts. In spite of the compact and intimate character of
our society the rehearsals were conducted with such secrecy
that we of the audience were not even aware of the name
of the show, until we received our programs as we took our
seats in the mess hall which had been requisitioned for a
theater. We unrolled our large five page programs to learn
that we were about to see the " Midnight Follies of the
Antarctic." The illusion that we were in a theater was
faithfully carried out in the programs. One had the same
difficulty picking out information about the show itself,
from the great mass of advertising, that he might have
experienced with a New York theater program.

First there were several specialty or vaudeville acts which
were very well received. Then came the main part of the
show which was a curious combination of musical comedy
chorus and Negro minstrels. The cast included Helen of
Troy, Cleopatra, Sappho, and Salome. I am sure that
Freddy Crockett was Cleopatra. Everyone agreed that he
was probably the handsomest woman who had ever been
in the Antarctic. And, curiously enough, mild mannered
Eddie Goodale was the hardest looking lady of the lot. I
think his name should have been Jezebel. The wigs made
of rope and the gowns made of towels — in fact the whole
make-up was a great credit to those who " put on the
show." But when the chorus began to sing we realized that
they had not been selected for any particular vocal ability.

The whole program reached a fitting climax in the dialogue which was bandied about by the Negro minstrels.

" Bones," said the Interlocutor Norman Vaughan, " Why for do you reckon Russell Owen is so bow-legged? "

" Well," replied Bones (Mike Thorne) , " I reckon that the weight of all the clothes he wears is just so great that his legs can't hold it up."

Nobody enjoyed this jibe more than Russell. He had an almost uncanny ability for completely obscuring himself in his various and sundry fur garments and was always being mildly " kidded " for his great ability to stand the cold.

When quiet was restored Mike came to the front of the stage with a bucket full of cold water. He pushed his head completely under the water and held it for several seconds and then came up for air. He did this repeatedly until everyone was completely mystified. Finally the Interlocutor asked him what he was doing.

" Why," he answered, " I am practicing diving so I can go with Larry on his 25 year old submarine."

For days I had been the butt for many good-humored jokes because I had indicated my intention of going on a proposed submarine trip across the Arctic. (Not the Wilkins Expedition.)

But there was one last quip that literally brought the house down.

One of the men was wearing a great big tin medal. The Interlocutor asked him what it was.

" That," he replied, " is a Causa Medal."

" What do you mean a Causa Medal — how did you get it? "

" Oh, I got that cause I didn't jump overboard when the barrier broke."

It will be remembered that when we were unloading supplies from the ships onto the barrier or the edge of the shelf ice, a great piece broke off nearly overturning one of the ships and dumping one man into the icy water. In their eagerness to help, a number of men unnecessarily jumped overboard. We had to put over an extra boat to rescue the rescuers. It was inevitable that this incident should provoke a good deal of friendly " kidding."

A man's most important asset, if he would keep his poise in such an intimate society as ours, is a sense of humor. The sooner a man learns to laugh at his own short-comings and peculiarities the better off will he be for he can be very sure that everyone else is going to do so.

It is inevitable that little personal traits or characteristics that would pass unnoticed elsewhere appear disproportionately large under such conditions. The very manner in which a man butters his bread or eats his soup may become an almost maddening thing and one needs outlet for such feelings. Our home talent shows furnished the necessary mediums for this — they were excellent safety valves, for in the dialogue, that was always a part of them, people were often reminded of their short-comings and under such circumstances had to take it. Only there could one say things, and be forgiven for them, that he could not say under normal or ordinary conditions.

There was one other institution that might be called a source of recreation or entertainment and that was the phonograph. We had two of these instruments but fortunately only one was in the Administration Building where I lived; the other was in the Biltmore or the Norwegian

House. Even so, one was far too many, for we had only a few good records. Someone would stroll over from the mess hall after breakfast and decide that he wanted to hear some music. He would play all the records and then go home. Shortly another would come in and decide to entertain himself in the same way. This was not necessarily bad for those who did not live and work in the Administration Building. But there were many days when we who did live there, had to listen to these same records fully a dozen times. Nothing is so beautiful that it will stand endless repetition and I am glad that we at least did not have Schubert's Unfinished Symphony. I think, though, that Dr. Coman and I would have stowed it away rather than let it be so abused. Dana did have a few records hidden away and it was an event when he brought out a new one. We stopped everything to listen.

Strom was the only man who made any attempt to play any kind of instrument. He had an accordion which he played with real charm, but this got into a bad state of repair early in the winter. Two or three times Arthur Walden sang us some of his songs of the Alaskan trails. Otherwise there was no music in Little America. No one else made any serious attempt to sing, and not once was any effort made to develop any chorus singing. This still seems a bit unusual in a group as large as ours. But I suspect that the absence of mediocre amateurish efforts to make music was a great factor in making for peace among us.

Perhaps you will best understand how we lived and divided our day if you follow me for a typical day's activity.

At 7 o'clock Pete Demas comes into the Administration

Building, closes the door, and then builds a fire. Then he goes over to the mess hall, starts a fire in the kitchen range and calls the cook. If I am not awake he calls me shortly after 8. Bernt, whose bunk is beside mine, gets up with me. It is still pretty cold even near the stove. The thermometer at the foot of Bill Haines' bunk indicates that the temperature was down to 22 degrees below zero last night here in the house. It is scarcely up to zero yet and the water in the bucket on top of the stove is quite solid. Bernt and I will have to go to breakfast without washing our hands. We are dressed and ready to go over to the mess hall at 8:30 and I call Commander Byrd and all the other men in the Administration Building just before we leave.

Since the weather is fairly good Bernt and I decide to go over the top. On the way we stop at the thermometer shelter and find that the lowest temperature last night was 72 degrees below zero and the alcohol still registers well below 60. We were always guessing the temperatures among ourselves but we rarely hit them correctly. One may easily feel warmer when the thermometer tells him it is 60 below zero if there is no wind than he will at 30 below zero if there is a good stiff breeze. It is the wind that makes Antarctic weather so formidable.

There are a few early risers in the mess hall who sit down to breakfast with us; Czegka, Dean Smith, and Strom never had to be called. Too often the others and the boys in the Norwegian House have to be routed out. Sometimes I wait hopefully until after breakfast to call the occupants of the latter place hoping they will bestir themselves, but they rarely do.

Breakfast over Bernt and I return to our part of town. If anyone here is still in bed then it is my custom to

" help" him get up. I also have to " drive" the men out
to work when there is any to be done. Once in the midst
of my threatenings and exhortations to get something
done Jack O'Brien called me " Simon Legree, the
slave driver" and " Simon" I remained throughout the
expedition.

Breakfast is finally over and by 10 o'clock everyone has
had time for his morning smoke. Captain McKinley and
Joe Rucker are already at work in the photographic laboratory. Tom Mulroy is at the task of filling the lamps with
gasoline. Haines and Harrison are inflating a balloon getting ready for an observation; Hanson is busy with his os-
cillograph in his laboratory; Commander Byrd and Charlie
Lofgren are closeted in the Commander's room going over
radiograms; Taffy is putting on all the clothes he can find
preparatory to a sojourn out in his snow house — his is the
most unpleasant task of all; Russell Owen is already
pounding away at his typewriter in the library: Van is
scratching his head as he thinks out some better way to
get a particular movie shot he wants; Quin Blackburn who
is sort of homeless, in that he sleeps in a snow house adjacent to the radio shack, has brought his " knitting" into
the library for the day. Quin became such an expert at
mending and darning socks and sweaters that he had more
business than he could easily attend to.

Probably the first man in camp to be at work is our
sixty-seven-year-old tailor, Martin Ronne. Ronne had
spent a summer in the Antarctic with Amundsen in 1910–
1911, and had later been with him three years in the Arctic.
It was Amundsen who had recommended him to Commander Byrd for this expedition. In spite of his years
there was no more youthful spirit among us than Martin.

He was always cheerful, and if asked for the reason invariably replied:

"Work, work, give me plenty work."

On all too rare occasions he was reminiscent of the years he had spent under Amundsen's command. He had a most profound respect for the ability of this lost leader of his, but this respect seemed not to have dampened his sense of humor. The prodigious size of Amundsen's nose seems to have been a never ending source of delight to him. He declared that Amundsen had the biggest nose in the world and pointed with pride to a crude sketch he had once made of it, and which had amused Amundsen so much that he had included it in one of his books.

I shall busy myself to-day working on charts to be used on our sledge journey.

Over in the mess hall Tennant and his assistant Clark are getting food ready to be cooked for supper. The breakfast litter has been cleared off the table and gathered about one end of it are June, Bubier, and Roth devising some kind of gadget for the airplanes. The other end is piled high with various kinds of foods where Blackie, Jack Bursey, and Joe de Ganahl are weighing and packing it for use on the trail. In a corner near the door Mike Thorne, Jack O'Brien, Norman Vaughan, Eddie Goodale, and Freddy Crockett are busily molding dog pemmican into little brickets for use on the trail. Each bricket will be one dog's portion or ration for a day. Dean Smith has become so proficient at his radio that he is copying press dispatches broadcast from New York.

Czegka is pounding away at a piece of aluminum getting it into shape for a part of the cooker he is building for our use on the trail. In a few minutes he may, with

Cold

EXACT REPLICA (BY STROM) OF THE STROM-
BALCHEN SLEDGES

equal facility, be repairing the delicate mechanism of somebody's watch.

Paul Siple, who sometimes finds a corner in which he can dissect his penguins in the mess hall, has been forced clear outside and is working to-day in an improvised laboratory of his own design, consisting of a snow house roofed over with a lifeboat. I am much interested in Paul's work for occasionally he finds a penguin stomach with small pebbles in it. This is of great interest to me for the penguin, being a meat-eating bird, has no gizzard; the stones in the stomach are doubtless accidental. Anyhow it is a unique way for me to add to my rock collection, and who knows but that these penguins may not have thus inadvertently brought me important information about coast lines that have never been seen?

Others who have not found any specific tasks are piled up in Benny Roth's bunk watching the rest at work, doubtless making remarks at them, or possibly discussing anything from prohibition to the shipping board.

Bernt Balchen and Sverre Strom have appropriated Blubberheim for a sledge factory, and are now hard at work lashing together one of the sledges that is destined to do such good work for us on our southward journey. They take so much of the limited space in this tiny house that Arthur Walden is crowded into his bunk where he sits reading " Kim." In a cramped corner is Chris Braathen building a miniature replica of the " City of New York."

At one o'clock there is a general lull when many of the boys stop for a bit of lunch and a cup of coffee. Then if the day turns out clear a good number will get out of doors for a little exercise. Commander Byrd misses few such opportunities to take a walk. The rest of us take our exercise practicing on skis. This is most important for those of us who are to make the sledge journeys, for we must plan to travel all the way on skis. On rare occasions Bernt goes out with me and gives me valuable pointers.

With four o'clock the work day officially ends, except for the " students " of the " University of Antarctica " which assembles after supper, but of course attendance here is purely optional. Our dining table is far too small for our large group. Not more than 16 can conveniently eat at one sitting. The result is that only those who come last are allowed any great leisure in which to finish their food. If one gets a seat at the first table and has good ears he can, from time to time, hear pointed remarks about his appetite and his general demeanor from those standing about waiting their turn.

Dinner over we are off to our games, our classes, or the library to read. " Taps " comes at 10 o'clock. The main lights are turned out, and then comes the one time of quiet during the waking hours in Little America. Though we all get into bed few of us go right to sleep. Most of us have provided ourselves with candles or some sort of individual light, and we look forward to the luxury of an hour or two of reading in bed before it gets so cold that we have to stop. The doors are opened at 11 o'clock and the frosty air seems to leap in. To read any longer I have to put on a hat and don some thin gloves but to-night I am reading again James Stephens' " Crock of Gold " and I can't stop now.

As the cold air creeps upward and displaces the warm, the lights go out here and there and before midnight the room is quite dark, but it is not still. There are a few noisy sleepers, and to-night the wind has sprung up and as

it sweeps across our tiny chimneys, which project up above
the house, it sets up a sound much like the deep tones of
an organ. It is rather restful.

Though there was a fairly even tenor to our days there
were always little things happening that served as variety.
Of course the weather was a perennial source of interest.
To our surprise it showed a much greater variety than we
had suspected it would. It was not uniformly extremely
cold. Every month during the year but one the thermometer rose to zero degrees Fahrenheit, and likewise every
month it descended below zero. The coldest month was
July with an average temperature of *minus 44.7 degrees*
and the warmest month was January with an average temperature of *plus 20.8 degrees*. The mean or average for a
continuous twelve months was *minus 12.7 degrees*. The
only mean annual temperature ever recorded that com-
pares with this is that recorded by Amundsen at Framheim, which was of course essentially in the same locality
we were in. Framheim was Amundsen's winter quarters
before he made his great sledge journey to the South
Pole.

The most abrupt changes in temperatures accompanied
blizzards. On more than one occasion we found the temperature rising as much as 60 degrees over night as the
winds increased. On at least two occasions, though the
thermometer recorded a temperature many degrees below
freezing, we had heavy fogs. It was a wet mist too — and
felt just as wet as a fog in the temperate latitudes might.
On June 11th such a fog was so pronounced that Haines
and Harrison called it " rain " — yet the air temperature
was more than 20 degrees below freezing. This particular
fog or mist left great deposits of long feathery crystals of

frost or rime on almost all solid objects. These crystals collected on the faces of objects turned toward the breeze.

In spite of all our precautions the dogs furnished us altogether too much variety. We thought our tunnels would solve the problem of preserving peace among them, but we had not reckoned on the zeal and intensity with which dogs are apt to pursue their love ambitions. No matter how gentle and mild a dog may ordinarily be, when he is occupied with the problem of courting a lady's favor there is no limit to the violence and ruthlessness with which he tries to overcome all opposition. It was well nigh impossible to keep some of the dogs chained; Rowdy, our very mildest dog, chewed holes through his wooden crate as though it were made of cardboard. Not until we had lost several of our best dogs in fights among themselves, did we completely realize the necessity of building a separate tunnel for the bitches, some distance removed from the rest.

The bitches beheld this sort of warfare with the utmost calmness. So far as they were concerned the best dog in the fight was always the favorite, but they became different creatures when they began to give birth to their puppies. They were extremely jealous of each other's progeny. We had to put them far apart else when one mother had absented herself a rival might come along and chew the heads off all her puppies. One of our best and friendliest bitches, Holly, chewed the heads off Amy Lowell's pups when they were several weeks old and were running around out of doors.

Nevertheless these huskies were the friendliest dogs I have ever seen. I have never known dogs more responsive to kindly treatment; just a word of friendly greeting to one and he would go into the most elaborate contortions to express his joy. And he was jealous of any attention given to any other dog. They sensed those who liked them and those who did not and were correspondingly responsive. They seemed to have an uncanny way of understanding the slightest change of tone in one's voice or at times even in one's looks.

But this man induced veneer of civilization seemed pretty thin in their attitude toward each other. It took little incentive for the primal instincts to break through. We never found it safe to let our dogs run loose without being closely watched. They welcomed the slightest excuse for a fight, and once a fight had started it had to be stopped with all possible haste else some of the dogs were apt to be killed outright or badly mutilated. This wolfish instinct occasionally cropped out even in the puppies. They were poor sports. Once a dog got down, even in play, the rest were apt to suddenly turn savage and tear him to pieces, especially if he happened to be from a different litter. But these same dogs might have but a moment before been the best of friends. Possibly these huskies might assume the same savage attitude toward man if he were down, though it is hard for me to believe this. On many occasions I have found myself all tangled up with them and rolled on the snow beneath them without ever suspecting any such attention on their part. As a matter of fact I do not think they are ever any more savage toward each other than would other dogs be were they herded together in such large packs.

Water was not easily had, especially in the Administration Building, where our supply was derived from melting snow in buckets on top of the little stoves. It was easy to become careless about the simplest matters of personal cleanliness. One might watch the water buckets religiously all day, keeping them filled with snow that he might have them full for a bath at night after " taps " when nobody would bother him. More often than not he would get undressed for the luxury of a bath only to find his bucket filled with dirty socks; somebody had appropriated it for washing clothes.

We had a very tricky collapsible rubber bath tub, just large enough in diameter so that one could sit in it with legs crossed if he were careful. The sides were quite unstable but kept their upright position if one did not lean against them. But until one got used to its eccentricities he might get into the tub and get himself all covered with soap and then find that he had gotten too near the edge of the tub and had let all the water run out. No matter, there was no more water to be had.

One day a man came to Dr. Coman with some minor ailment; the doctor examined him and in doing so noticed that his nails were in " deep mourning " and his hands rather dusky.

" Well," he said, with a twinkle in his eye, " from the looks of your nails and the gray color coming over your skin I should say that you had the ' Antarctic disease.' "

Ever after if one became too careless in the matter of personal cleanliness his case was apt to be quite publicly diagnosed as this dread disease. He had to submit to the best known treatment — soap and water. As a matter of fact, so excellent was the health of the men that this was about the only ailment that Dr. Coman was ever called upon to diagnose.

In a group as large as ours there were, of course, some

whose attitudes might conceivably have been considered
a little over polite and even obsequious toward Commander Byrd. It was inevitable that someone should point
out that such an attitude was dictated from motives of self
interest. And thus the terms " flag waving " and " apple
rubbing " were invented. If one were too obvious in his
courtesy toward the Commander he was accused by his
fellows of being guilty of one of the two above offenses.
All this was in the best of humor and without venom, but
still there were some who found it so difficult to stand
even a mild amount of " twigging " as Taffy called it, that
they were discouraged from being as polite as they should
have been.

So varied were our tastes and trades, that whenever a
group of half a dozen men or so were gathered one might
linger about the fringe of it and be rewarded by comments naïvely philosophic and even original. Quin Blackburn, whose love for big words and involved construction,
but who was quite correct in their use, was a delight to us
all. Chips Gould was equally fond of big words, but usually demonstrated a curious uncertainty as to their meaning. One night these two men were partners in a bridge
game. After they had played a long time with little success
Quin said:

" It is a curious fact, but I seem to have had mediocre
hands all the evening."

" Well," said Chips, " then you had better get some
kerosene and wash it off."

On another occasion Quin was telling someone that one
of the bitches in his team was about to have pups and that
the loss of the dog would weaken the team. Only Quin
phrased it thus:

" I fear that the probability of impending motherhood is going to mar seriously the efficiency of my team." There was no more genial nature among us than Quin. He was a good expeditioner.

I believe the most important single source of recreation that made the time pass easily was our library — the Layman Library — of some 3000 volumes. When we were looking forward toward the winter night all of us anticipated great times with the books, but few of us, I think, had such ambitious projects as did one man who came to me one day early in the winter and said:

" Larry, do you know what I am going to do during this winter night? " Of course I hadn't the slightest idea.

" Well," he said, " I am going to learn aerial surveying and navigation and read the Encyclopedia Britannica through."

It seemed a fairly ambitious program to me, but I didn't want to discourage the man so I assured him that if he carried out the project he would certainly achieve the essentials of a liberal education. His literary aspirations were rather short lived. He did start with volume I, letter A of the encyclopedia and got as far as " ammonium tetrachloride " — I saw him throw the book down with a look of disgust and asked him what was the matter.

" The stuff in that d—— book is no good for an aviator," he replied.

Commander Byrd had charged me with the responsibility of collecting the library as part of our preparations back in New York. I asked him what sort of books he especially liked to read. His reply indicated considerable catholicity of taste.

" Dickens, detective stories, and philosophy."

And of all the various classes of reading matter that were represented detective stories were the most widely read, with accounts of other polar expeditions making a close second. The most widely read single book of all was W. H. Hudson's " Green Mansions." Donn Byrne and Joseph Lincoln were more exhaustively read than any other two authors — Mark Twain came next. We had a complete set of Kipling's works which was scarcely touched. As for myself, had the winter night given me opportunity for no other reading than Romain Rolland's " Jean Christophe " and Galsworthy's " Forsyte Saga " in its entirety I should still have considered it well spent. To me these are two works of this day that will live if any do. " Jean Christophe " is the most satisfying work of art with which I have ever come face to face.

I look through my diary in vain for any indications that the winter night lagged. It seemed to hurry on. I do find myself ever coming back to comment upon how beautiful, how varied, and how clean and withal how different it all was. On Saturday June 23rd I find this entry:

" Outside to-day it is calm and dark and still — so very still. When there is no wind this is a land of unparalleled quiet. But it is a different quiet than one feels back home. I have stood in the woods at home when the world seemed dead. There was no kind of sound. But in that world where a variety of sound was the rule rather than the exception such a silence was oppressive if not ominous. Not so here — this is a land of silence. One stands in the midst of it without any feeling of oppressiveness. It is an expanding sort of silence. It is inviting. It is the natural state here and I like it — I have come to feel at home in the midst of it.

" And what a varied and colorful world this all becomes when there are no clouds. I long ago ceased to miss the objects that are so much a part of a landscape at home. I think I have at times even forgotten that there were such things as trees and grass and flowers — not that the sight of these things will be less wonderful and arresting when I see them again — but this is a different world entirely — it is a new world to me and in its way is complete and satisfying. Nature paints the ice and snow and the clouds with colors so rich that the picture is complete in itself. In the light of the moon and the stars it is a pastel sort of world. In the brilliant light of the long summer it was sharp and clear cut — things had sharp corners that now have but graceful curves. There are no sharp night shadows. The beauty lies in the gradations of color."

There were few stretches of clear weather when we did not have some kind of auroral display. Most often it was manifested as huge greenish white curtains or arches. Sometimes these would be quite still for some seconds but more often they were dancing — sometimes with the complete ecstasy and abandonment of jazz and again with the slow writhing motion of the oriental dance. From a dark center overhead I have seen streamers shooting outward in all directions, like the spokes of a wheel, until they disappeared below the horizon on all sides. I have watched a great wave of faint red to purple light boil up over the dark rim of the night, way off toward the northeast, and then rise higher and higher until the whole heavens were filled with the " wondrous light " and even the great stretches of snow all about me shimmered with a pale abalone glow.

I should be sorry for anyone who could watch an Antarctic night in all its varied splendor and beauty — its restless aurora, its blazing stars and white moon — and not realize that he had had full compensation for any privation or hardship it had cost him to come.

But the Antarctic night is not always beautiful. Too often thick layers of clouds hide all this, and then the sky is just as pitchy as one can find any where in the world, then " The icy earth swung blind and blackening in the moonless air."

And I think there are few things in nature more nearly approaching the weird or terrifying than a thorough going blizzard when it is so dark. The whining and screeching of the wind as it sucks itself across the snow, that one cannot see, takes on a new note that is often ominous. One has no sense of direction in the swirling icy dust and dares not venture an arm's length beyond the shelter of the house.

One thing that surprised me about the night was the persistence of the glow of the hidden sun on our northern sky at noon time. Even in very midwinter when the sun was farthest north from us, when in fact its direct rays were right above Havana, Cuba, there was yet a pink glow at midday along our northern horizon that dispelled a bit of the darkness.

Really before we had any deep realization that the long night was about us, the sun had passed its farthest north point on June 21st and had started its journey southward again. It seemed to return by leaps and bounds. In the latter days of July it gave so much light that we were able to get out of doors a good deal — Commander Byrd to his walks and many of the rest of us on our skis.

I needed practice on my skis so badly that I often went out alone. It was always my habit to ski away from camp in the direction from which the wind came. Then if I found myself freezing I could turn about and ski back without any grave danger of serious frostbite. In such intense cold as we had during these days, it would have been easy to ski away from camp with the wind, farther than one realized; getting back against the wind might have caused serious freezing. Therefore my ski journeys radiated from camp as the wind direction varied. To be sure on the very coldest days, when the temperature was down to 50 or 60 below zero, there was rarely even a breeze so one could ski in whatever direction he wished.

Chapter III

HOW WE PLANNED TO DO IT

Prove all things; hold fast that which is good.

St. Paul

THE geological party together with the help of the supporting party was designed to serve the ends of the expedition in two distinct phases.

In the first place it was to proceed directly southward from Little America to the foot of the Queen Maud Mountains along the route over which the polar flight was to be made. En route, depots of dog food, man food and fuel, each containing supplies for at least three or four days for the geological party, were to be established as follows:

Depot Number 1	......	79 degrees	21 minutes south
" 2	 80	" 10	" "
" 3	 81	" 00	" "
" 4	 81	" 45	" "
" 5	 82	" 35	" "
" 6	 83	" 25	" "
" 7	 84	" 15	" "
" 8	 85	" 00	" "

These depots were not only for the use of the geological party on its way back to Little America, but for emergency use by the polar flight party. It was planned that depot number 8 would be the base for the polar flight, that we should have located there a good landing field; and that we should stand by with radio direction finder to assist the plane in locating the proposed field. It was further planned that the geological party would stand by at this depot until the polar flight was completed.

Our plans for field work in addition to our expected co-operation with the polar flight were made in the light of what we believed the geography of this sector to be, as revealed by Amundsen.

There were three things of potential geographical and geological importance that we hoped to be able to do. First — at the end of our southward trek to the foot of the Queen Maud Mountains, to climb Mt. Fridtjof Nansen in an attempt to get a cross section of the range. Second — to sledge eastward along the foot of the Queen Maud Mountains to its junction with the supposed Carmen Land. This was the most intriguing prospect of the whole summer for me, for Amundsen's plotted position of Carmen Land indicated a highland cutting off practically at right angles to the trend of the main Queen Maud Mt. structure. Such a relationship of two mountain ranges would have been unique. Thirdly — on our way northward to Little America, to leave the main trail at depot number 5 and explore the lands and "appearances of land" indicated by Amundsen as existent between latitudes 81 and 82. The map opposite page 70 illustrates these proposed plans.

To carry out all of the above plans, we estimated that we must expect to be away from our base at Little America for about three months. Accordingly our supplies were made up on the assumption that we should be in the field 90 days. We planned to dispose of these days as follows:

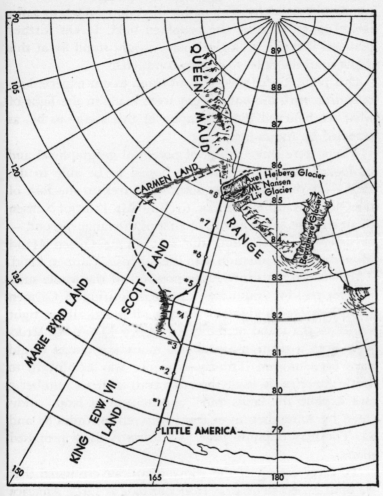

PROPOSED PLANS BASED UPON AMUNDSEN'S CHART

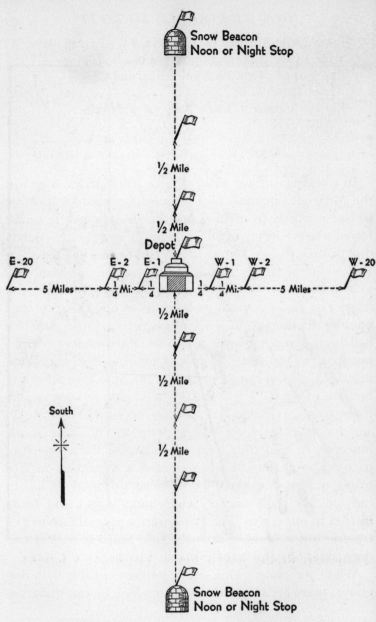

Snow Beacon
Noon or Night Stop

½ Mile

½ Mile

Depot

E - 20   E - 2 E - 1   W - 1 W - 2   W - 20

← 5 Miles → ¼ Mi. ¼ ← ¼ ¼ Mi. → ← 5 Miles →

½ Mile

½ Mile

½ Mile

South

Snow Beacon
Noon or Night Stop

PLAN FOR MARKING THE TRAIL

From Little America to depot No. 8 ...... 28 days
Stand by for polar flight at depot No. 8 .... 7 "
Exploration of Mt. Fridtjof Nansen and Car-
   men Land .... 32 "
Return journey to Little America with side
   trip .... 23 "
                                                   ―――――
      Total .... 90 days

In working out any kind of time schedule for travel in the Antarctic one must take account of possible delays due to bad weather. In making out the above schedule we allowed a safety factor of 20 per cent for unavoidable delays due to such things, but as it turned out, we lost less than 10 per cent of our time in the field due to such causes.

The success of our whole program depended upon the dogs. The first summer's work of unloading the ships and hauling all the supplies across the ice to Little America had been gruelling work for them. Furthermore we did not have an unlimited supply of mature dogs, and Commander Byrd did not think it wise for us to take all of the best ones with us. He thought it advisable to keep two or three teams in Little America for necessary work there, and for emergency use. We had the use of these teams, however, in that they were the teams of the supporting party. The geological party needed a minimum of five teams, of nine dogs each. To make up this total we had to include five pups scarcely eight months old and three bitches in our teams. The latter were a potential source of trouble but we had to take the risk. Scarcely half of our dogs could be considered first rate.

When one plans a long sledge journey entirely with dog power, there are two main ways in which he can make use of the dogs. First he can plan to gauge his travelling and field work with the expectation of bringing all of the dogs back alive. To cover a great distance from the main base by this plan it is necessary to advance supplies by re-laying. In other words the weight of food, fuel and equipment combined would make a total way beyond that which the dogs could haul at one time. Therefore a part of the supplies are hauled ahead and then the teams return for the remainder. It is at once apparent that in the mere matter of reaching his objective by this method one must travel over much of the route three times. This in itself is an objection in that it necessitates the consumption of large quantities of food and supplies; but of much greater importance is the fact that such a method is bound to be relatively slow. The field season in the Antarctic is at best all too brief. The brevity of the time at our disposal in which to accomplish the things we had projected, had to be a most important factor in formulating any plans.

The second plan for using dogs exclusively on a journey as long as we hoped to make, is one that no one can contemplate with any cheer. It is making good one's journey by sacrificing the weakest dogs as one proceeds. The dogs become pawns in a game and the fittest survive the longest. This method makes it unnecessary to carry food for so many dogs all the way to one's goal. A great lightening of loads is thus possible. Of equal importance is the fact that, though he sometimes takes to it with reluctance, the husky is an accommodating creature, in that he will eat the carcasses of his dead companions and they seem to be good food for him. Thus killing the dogs en route accomplishes the two fold end of reducing very greatly the amount of dog food that must be taken in the first place, and by the addition of the dog carcasses, it greatly augments the supply on hand.

To have achieved the purposes of our trip by the first method, we should have been obliged to carry an additional 3000 pounds of dog food, and it would have necessitated a field season at least a half longer than we had at our disposal. There was not even a possibility of succeeding by this method. A dog could not haul a sufficient weight of food for himself all the way to the mountains and back for the time we expected to be gone, much less deliver any pay load. We had no alternative except to make our plans according to the second method. Yet even as we made these plans we did not think it would be necessary to carry them out in their entirety for Commander Byrd had assured us that if it were feasible, he would have the planes fly out from Little America and drop dog food to us. This hope always lurked in the backs of our minds as we went about completing our plans.

Norman Vaughan whose special responsibility on the trip was to be the dogs worked out the following schedule for their disposal.

From Little America to Depot
  No. 5 .... 5 teams (45 dogs) — 17.5 days
From Depot No. 5 to Depot
  No. 8 .... 5 " (40 ") — 10.5 "
For Polar Flight Wait ...... 4 " (28 ") — 7 "
For Explorations .... 3 " (21 ") — 32 "
For return to Little America 3 " (21 ") — 23 "

This schedule meant that upon our arrival at depot No. 5 we should have to kill five dogs; at No. 8 twelve more would have to die, and immediately after the polar flight was over and the possibility that we might have to turn ourselves into a rescue party had passed, we would have to kill seven more.

As we turned our attention to the details of gathering our supplies together and perfecting our equipment, we drew upon the experiences of those who had preceded us in this kind of travel. Nansen, Peary, Stefansson and Rasmussen made their contributions from the Arctic; but of course of much greater value to us were the records of Scott, Shackleton, Mawson and Amundsen. Since we expected to cover a route that had in part been pioneered by Amundsen and might therefore in large measure meet the same obstacles that he faced, his book " The South Pole " was our most valuable source of information. And, as a matter of fact, in the task of making careful and adequate preparations, and carrying through his project to a successful conclusion, I do not think anybody has ever surpassed Amundsen's journey to the South Pole and return. In the matter of pluck and resourcefulness, I think Shackleton's near approach (111 miles) to the South Pole in 1908–1909, and his successful return to his base at McMurdo Sound, will stand perhaps for all time as one of the greatest triumphs of the human will over nature in her most forbidding aspects.

Perhaps the most prolific source of trouble and the commonest cause of failure, at least on the earlier sledging journeys, was improper food. In devising a ration for a journey as extended as we expected ours to be, there were several guiding factors that we did not let ourselves forget or neglect. In the first place we had to get the greatest food value we could for the minimum weight (throughout all the details of our preparations even to such tiny items as a toothbrush, that old bugbear of weight could

Up the Radio Towers for First Glimpse of Returning Sun

not be neglected) and withall have a balanced ration which would contain sufficient " roughage " and would be anti-scorbutic, that is would contain the necessary vitamin C which prevents that most dreaded of polar maladies, scurvy. Secondly this ration should be composed of foods that would need little or no cooking. We had to carry all of our fuel, and fuel is heavy. Thirdly, so far as possible, some variation in the ration was highly desirable.

With these notions in the background and largely due to the advice of Dr. Coman, the following ration was worked out:

Food item	Daily ration per man	1 man for 90 days	6 men for 90 days
Pemmican	8 oz.	45 lbs.	270.00 lbs.
Biscuits	10	56.25	337.50
Sugar	4	22.50	135.00
Powdered milk	4	22.50	135.00
Oatmeal	2	11.25	67.50
Chocolate	2	11.25	67.50
Soup meal sausages .	2	11.25	67.50
Tea	0.5	2.81	17.00
Bacon	1.33	7.50	45.00
Butter	0.59	3.33	20.00
Peanut butter	0.29	1.64	10.00
Malted milk	0.74	4.17	25.00
Cocoa	0.14	0.83	5.00
Salt			4.00
Pepper			1.00
Lemon powder			9.00
Matches and toilet paper			12.00
Totals	35.69 oz.	200.39 lbs.	1228.00 lbs.

The first group in the above list furnished the bulk or fuel part of our food, while the second furnished the desired variety. Furthermore the lemon powder was highly anti-scorbutic. It is of interest to compare the weight of our daily ration per man with that of other explorers:

Greely	36	oz
McClintock	42	"
Peary	36.5	"
Nares	40	"
Abruzzi	43.5	"
Scott	34.7	"
Shackleton	34.82	"
Mawson	34.25	"

Some of the above items, perhaps, need a little explanatory comment. The pemmican was of Danish manufacture and the same kind that Amundsen had used with such success. It is composed essentially of finely ground dried beef and fats with a little seasoning. One pound is supposed to be the equivalent in food value of six or seven pounds of raw beef. The biscuits were in themselves a very good food, for they contained in addition to the natural wheat content, other vegetables and some meat. I found them more durable than edible — but strangely enough the former quality is a most essential one. If these biscuits were of the same consistency as ordinary soda crackers, they would get badly broken up and ground into powdery crumbs in the heavy handling they have to undergo. Considerable loss would be inevitable and it would be increasingly difficult to make an exactly equitable distribution or division into individual rations. The soup meal sausages were of the long famed German " erbswurst " variety and made a most valuable and welcome addition to the pemmican.

Of all the food items on the above list, the only one that really needs a good deal of cooking is oatmeal. One might at first thought assume that the amount of fuel necessary to cook the oatmeal would be so great that to take it along would be poor judgment. But we found that a large vacuum jug made an excellent fireless cooker and that it was only necessary to bring the oatmeal to a boil and then pour it into the jug after supper at night and leave it until morning. No matter whether it was 15 degrees above zero or 30 below, we always had steaming hot oatmeal for breakfast. Again the question arises as to whether the luxury of oatmeal for breakfast justifies the addition of so great a weight to our loads as the vacuum jug. Had the jug served no other purpose we would not have let ourselves be persuaded to take it. But we worked out a scheme for travelling whereby it much more than made up for its weight, by the great amount of fuel it saved in other lines. We knew that we might be travelling anywhere from six to sixteen hours per day and that our loads would be so heavy that we could not at any time ride on the sledges. We realized that we had to plan to travel all the way on skis. Under such conditions it seemed very unwise to attempt a whole day of travelling without something to drink, at least. But the business of unlashing a loaded sledge and putting up a tent at noon time, so that we could have our stove lighted to melt snow for water, would have taken up a great deal of time and would have greatly increased our fuel consumption. The vacuum jug saved us all this trouble. After breakfast, while the cooker was still hot, we brewed a jug of hot tea, cocoa or malted milk. Thus we were able to stop for our noon day lunch and have two or three cups of some kind of hot drink, without causing much delay on the march.

We planned to distribute our ration through the three meals of the day as follows:

BREAKFAST
2 mugs of oatmeal with sugar and milk
2 biscuits
2 cups of tea with sugar and milk

LUNCH
1 four ounce bar of chocolate
2 biscuits with butter or peanut butter
2 ounces of pemmican (to eat cold)
2 cups of tea with lemon powder and sugar, or cocoa or malted milk

SUPPER
6 ounces of pemmican made into hot stew or " hoosh " with soup meal sausage
4 biscuits with butter, peanut butter or bacon fat
2 cups of tea, cocoa or malted milk
2 slices (thick) of bacon

Finally as a measure of convenience we packed our food supplies in bags; the pemmican and biscuits in bags, each containing rations for one day for the whole party, and the less bulky items like sugar in bags containing rations for one week. We made many of the heavy cloth bags, that I was taking for keeping my prospective rock samples separate, do double duty. We filled them with supplies that we expected to consume before we reached the mountains — that is, before they would be needed to hold rock specimens.

The right kind of dog food was no less important than the right kind of man food. The biscuits which had been made for this purpose had proved unsatisfactory. Fortunately this discovery was made before the dogs reached New Zealand, but we had only a very limited time in which to find some substitute. Dr. Malcolm of the University of Otago, Dunedin, came to our assistance and devised for us a well-balanced dog food which had the additional advantage of being of the compactness of pemmican. The Hudson Chocolate Company turned over its entire plant and personnel without charge to manufacture this food for us. Of course this was a new and untried produce and we did not know whether it would be entirely successful but it proved to be better than we had even hoped for. Throughout our long trek the dogs maintained their fondness for it, kept healthy on it and did abundant work from it. I think no more valuable contribution, in the way of preparations, to the ultimate success of the expedition was made than this.

To avoid any losses that might result from chopping this " pemmican " up when we were on the trail and also to make our work easier we warmed it up in the mess hall during the winter night and then molded it into little brickets each of which weighed a pound and a half which was a dog's portion for a day.

In the matter of our personal equipment we made the same mistake that most other sledge travellers, and especially amateurs, had at first made in the Antarctic. We took more than we needed. Our personal kit for three months, including the clothing that we would be wearing at any time, consisted of: 1 fur parka, 1 pr. fur pants (optional, most of us took none) , 1 woolen parka, 1 pr. woolen pants,

1 windproof parka, 2 pr. windproof pants, 1 pr. heavy canvas pants (optional) , 1 windproof shirt, 2 woolen shirts, 2 suits of woolen underwear, 1 woolen sweater, 1 fur hat, 1 woolen helmet, 1 woolen scarf, 2 prs. mukluks, 1 pr. ski boots, 1 pr. very large canvas boots, 2 prs. caribou socks, 1 pr. moccasins, 8 pr. woolen socks, 2 pr. heavy oversocks, 2 pr. felt inner soles, 2 pr. windproof socks, 1 pr. fur mitts with liners, 2 pr. canvas or leather mitts with woolen liners, 2 pr. extra mitt liners, 1 pr. windproof cuffs, 1 towel, 1 sewing kit, 1 toilet kit, 1 sheath knife, 2 pr. snow glasses, senna grass and 1 sleeping bag.

One has no notion of just how great a part of the bodily waste is dissipated as perspiration until he has tried sledging in the Antarctic. He must wear clothing that will " breathe," that is clothing that will, so far as possible, let the perspiration escape. Even so when the temperature is very low the air will absorb scarcely any moisture, and in spite of all possible precautions one's clothing does get damp. Whenever one stops for a rest, after he has been working hard, he must don a heavy parka at once to keep from getting chilled. I put my fur parka on but once during the whole sledge trip, for I found a heavy woolen one with a windproof cover over it to be quite sufficient.

At no time, no matter how cold it got, did most of us find it wise to wear fur clothing when we were sledging along. There was no way to keep the perspiration from our bodies from collecting on the inside of the parka or the pants, with the result that in a fairly short time, these would take on all the characteristics of a coat of mail. Even at temperatures of 40 degrees below zero we were surprised to discover that we needed relatively little clothing to keep warm as we skied along. Not more than three times in the course of our journey did I even need a sweater over my woolen shirt and underwear, beneath my windproof suit. Perhaps I should add, and with no intent to be facetious, that since I was so awkward on skis I got much more exercise and worked much harder to cover the same distance than would a person who could handle himself easily, as Mike Thorne and Freddy Crockett did. But under ordinary conditions, that is for sleeping or any quiet occupation, I got cold relatively easily.

If one can keep the wind out, and still allow some measure of the perspiration to dissipate from his body, the most difficult part of the task of keeping warm is solved. This is accomplished by wearing the above mentioned suit of windproof cloth on the outside of all the other clothing. Often we also wore windproof socks and a windproof shirt inside the parka. Good windproof cloth should be as light as possible, consistent with being strong and tightly woven. Most Antarctic explorers have used a very light Scotch gabardine, but we used a very closely woven long-fibered cotton cloth such as is used for covering fuselages of airplanes and found it very satisfactory. A whole suit of this material weighed less than two pounds.

In addition to its main purpose of cutting the wind, we found that if the weather were not too warm, so that we did not perspire too freely, the windproof clothing and especially the shirt and the socks, acted as collecting mediums or sort of blotters for the perspiration. When the moisture froze in this kind of cloth it could be shaken off or worked out much more easily than it could from heavy woolens.

All Antarctic clothing must be loosely fitting, and especially the windproof parka and pants. The pants looked as large and roomy as a Dutchman's trousers and had draw strings about the bottoms so that they could be tied up to keep out the snow. In general we found pockets in these outer garments to be a nuisance. Of course it is unhandy to be obliged to partially undress to get at one's handkerchief, but it is even more unpleasant to have exposed pockets that are forever filling with snow.

We promptly learned that the most vital parts of our bodies to be kept warm were our hands and feet. If we kept them warm and free from frostbites, we had little trouble otherwise. Here again we found it advisable to wear clothing that so far as possible would let the hands and feet " breathe." Sliding along and working the ski sticks with our hands made them perspire somewhat. We found that heavy woolen mitts with a windproof or canvas cloth outer mitt, that would allow some of the moisture at least to dissipate, were warmer than fur mitts.

If one is flying, or riding, or not doing physical labor, then of course there is no clothing so warm throughout as furs; one should have them. But when one works hard and perspires, the whole technique of keeping warm, as pointed out above, is changed.

It is impossible to devise footwear that will allow much dissipation of the moisture. Whether it be mukluks or ski boots, the leather is fairly impervious and the best one can do is to use green or untanned or at least unoiled leather. But one's feet and consequently his socks get wetter than any other part of the body or clothing. Our feet demanded the first attention when we stopped at the end of the day. We were indebted to Martin Ronne for saving us a good deal of misery in this respect. He made huge canvas boots for us with feet more than a foot long.

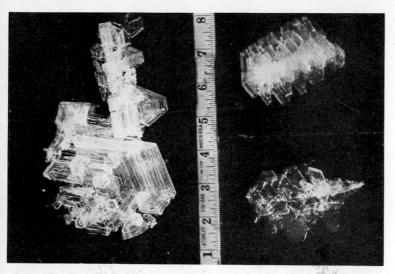

ICE CRYSTALS

ICE FLOWERS

A Crevasse Cave

These were of course very light and were not suited for travel, but, when partially filled with senna grass, were about the warmest footgear imaginable. It became our practice, when we stopped to make camp, to take off our ski boots and wet socks and put on the canvas boots before we did anything else. We kept our socks as dry as possible during the day by wearing two to four pairs of socks inside our boots, and lining the soles with felt insoles or senna grass. Senna grass has high absorbtive qualities and is very tough so it can be used over and over again, and it is more easily and more quickly dried than any kind of felt or cloth. The perspiration collects on it as rime or becomes such immediately on exposure to the air, and most of it can be shaken out.

Senna grass or its equivalent has been used from time immemorial by the Eskimos of Arctic America and by the nomads of northern Europe and it was from Lapland that our supply came.

Important as it is to travel with all possible comfort, it is even more vital that one should be able to keep warm and sleep well at night. We spent more time in " research " on the problem of finding the best kind of sleeping bag than on all others combined. After studying the results and reactions of other sledgers to two or three men bags, we concentrated our attention upon finding the best type of one man bag for our purpose. We profited most from Stefansson's methods and were familiar with Amundsen's advice that after trying all sorts of modifications he always came back to the simplest type of bag. Somehow all this did not in the least deter us from experimenting and finding out for ourselves. The one thing we did not need to experiment about was the material of which the bags were to be made. Nansen and Peary had settled that. Nothing has ever been found that is quite as satisfactory as reindeer skin. Reindeer skin is not covered with " fur " in the strict sense. It is covered with long hair but the hair is thicker than that of any other animal we know of. To be sure real fur such as one finds on a seal might of itself be warmer but this is entirely offset by the fact that hair like that of the reindeer is much more easily kept dry and hence for our kind of use is much warmer, for here, as in our clothing, if one can keep dry he can keep warm.

Many of the boys who were members of the sledging parties and several who were not, designed various modifications in their sleeping bags and then tested them out-of-doors. After listening to their comments and particularly those of Pete Demas who had so faithfully carried out his experiments, I was sure I could design the proper kind of bag. All of our bags were of the same general design in that they were shaped a good deal like an old-fashioned coffin — wide at the top to accommodate the shoulders and narrowing toward the feet.

Probably the greatest problem in designing the perfect sleeping bag comes from the fact that it must be so arranged that one's breath escapes into the open air and not into the bag, and yet so devised that the head is covered and kept warm. In my mind's eye I could see the ideal bag. I sewed my bag up completely then cut a hole about two feet in diameter across the top. I then sewed a strip of light fawn skin about two feet in width around this hole. I ran a puckering string around the free side of this strip. Thus I reasoned that I could get into the bag and pull the fawn skin tight around my neck with the puckering string. This would keep cold air out of the bag and would also cause my breath to keep out. Then I thought I could pull my head down inside the bag like a turtle and thus keep it warm.

It looked like such a good model that Blackie wanted to try it out. He did so one night, when the temperature was 65 degrees below zero. He had little to say about his experiences, but showed no inclination to make a second trial. Dr. Coman became curious, so I generously offered to let him try my invention. He too offered little comment about the kind of night he had spent but I could not fail to notice that he spent the major part of the following day asleep in his own bed inside the house. I was beginning to get a bit suspicious about the efficacy of my idea and decided to give the bag a trial indoors before sleeping outside in it. One trial was enough; I shivered all night in my bunk inside the house. The fawn skin neck arrangement was a total failure.

I made several other modifications without achieving the kind of bag I wanted. Finally I sewed the bag all up and then cut a slit clear across it, from one side to the other, about two feet from the top. Now it will be seen that I could easily get into the bag by putting my feet into the lower part and then drawing myself down far enough so that I could push my head and shoulders into or under the upper part which now functioned as a hood. The big slit let in too much air and my breath still largely remained in the bag. I next sewed a wide strip of the same kind of heavy skin of which the bag was made onto the lower side of this slit. This was a great improvement for now when I got into the bag I could pull this over my chest clear under my chin. The slit was thus closed to keep out the cold air, my head was covered, and my exhaled breath could not get down inside the bag. There was still one difficulty. The bag was hard to turn inside out and I knew this would have to be done frequently when we were out on the trail. I solved this difficulty by splitting the bag part way down the side below the hood part. To keep the cold air from coming in this slit, I again sewed a strip of heavy skin along one side. I then arranged toggles so that I could pull the bag together tightly after I got into it, but could loosen it with equal ease when it became necessary to turn it inside out. This bag really was very successful. I had little difficulty in keeping it dry and for the very coldest weather I got additional warmth by using a blanket bag inside this fur one, made by simply sewing together two sides and the bottom of a medium weight woolen blanket.

Though a number of different types of tents were tried out, we had almost decided ahead of time that it would be difficult to improve upon the kind we had used in the Rockefeller Mountains. It did not seem likely that we would ever experience such winds as our tent had withstood there. This was an " A " tent large enough to accommodate three men if they slept " contagious." Instead of the usual tent poles at either end to hold it up this tent had bamboo poles in each of the four corners. The bottoms of these poles projected six to eight inches below the tent floor and were fitted with sharp pegs. To put up the tent it was only necessary to push the pegged ends into the snow and then stretch the guy lines from either end. Around the whole tent floor, on the outside, was a skirt or flounce about one foot wide. Snow was piled onto this and not only kept the tent more stable but prevented cold winds from getting at us from underneath. The room inside could be further increased by staking out the two guys that were attached to each wall on the outside.

One of the most prolific sources of wetness inside a tent comes from the moisture that collects on the walls from cooking. Therefore instead of having two three men tents with separate messes in each, we decided to have a third tent which would be used exclusively for cooking. This meant an additional weight of 20 pounds, but it turned out to be a wise addition. Martin Ronne made two of the " Λ " type of tents for us to sleep in and we should have used a third one for cooking, but he had already made a square pyramidal one which we thought would be suitable or at least usable for this purpose and save him the trouble of making an additional tent. We did away, in part, with the difficulty of rime collecting inside the cook tent, by cutting a large vent in the top which we always had open when we were cooking, unless there was a blizzard.

The commonest source of moisture inside our sleeping tents was loose snow. Every precaution was taken to keep it out. We carried whisk brooms for each tent, and as far as possible brushed the loose snow off our clothing before we went in. We had flaps in the floors of the tent into which we could sweep any snow that we had inadvertently brought in. There is also danger of getting the tent wet through the floor. This danger is greater the higher the temperature. If the snow is a few degrees above zero the heat of one's body in his sleeping bag may be great enough to melt the snow or at least make it wet beneath him. Christopher Braathen solved this problem very satisfactorily in a novel way that we all immediately copied. From the thin ply wood which had been brought along to repair the wings of the Fokker, and which would never be of any use for this purpose since the loss of this plane in the Rockefeller Mountains, Braathen cut little slats about four inches wide. He sewed a number of these onto two narrow strips of canvas spacing the individual slats about two inches apart. The whole thing could be folded up into a tiny compact bundle but when unrolled was as long as the sleeping bag. This weighed but a pound and a half and yet when placed underneath the bag was sufficient to keep one from melting or thawing out the snow beneath him.

Perhaps no part of sledging operations has been given more attention than the best kind of sledge to use. For our kind of travel, experience had demonstrated that the idea was a long narrow sledge with wide ski-like wooden runners curved up at both ends — that is a double-ended sledge. Such a sledge is lashed together with rawhide thongs rather than being rigidly held with metal or wood. We ourselves found that a long narrow sledge like this had a much easier motion over the surface; there was much less jarring about over the irregularities. When such a sledge is loaded it sort of weaves its way over the snow. Except over a very rough surface, each part of the runner contacts with the snow so that the load is much more evenly distributed on the runner surface than is the case with a rigid sledge. The net result of all this is that the sledge does not sink so far into the snow, and, hence, pulls much more easily.

We were not entirely satisfied with our sledging equipment. The heavy rigid freight sledges and the basket sledges with which the expedition was equipped had been eminently suited to the heavy task of hauling all of our equipment and supplies from the two ships, across the rough ice to Little America; but they were unnecessarily

cumbersome and heavy for the long distance kind of travel
that we were anticipating. We had three flexibly built ski
runner sledges that Amundsen had sent over from Norway.
These had the disadvantage of being single-ended, i.e.
turned up only at one end, and were somewhat lighter
than we thought we needed. The double-ended sledge
makes for greater strength; it insures keeping the runners
convex which is most important; it glides along over rough
surfaces more smoothly, for there is no sharp end on the
rear to catch the sastrugi or other irregularities and bounce
the sledge about. But we decided to use these Norwegian
sledges for trailers behind the rigid freight sledges. We
still needed two more trailer sledges. Balchen and Strom
built two of the long narrow flexible ideal type for us,
which proved to be so sturdy, in spite of their light graceful lines, that we used them for lead sledges. I doubt if any
explorers ever had more perfect sledges than these two
" Strom-Balchen " sledges. Strom later made two light
trailer sledges using ordinary skis for runners so that when
we left Little America, we planned to have three freight
sledges and the two Strom-Balchen sledges for lead sledges
and the three Norwegian and two Strom ski sledges for
trailers.

We planned to carry our supplies on the sledges inside
heavy canvas tanks that were securely fastened to the
sledges, so that if they overturned, or fell into crevasses, we
should not lose our loads.

When driving along with the sledges, no matter how
good the surface may be, it is often necessary to have some
way of guiding and at least partially controlling them.
Amundsen and his companions had ropes tied to their
sledges for this purpose. I think Arthur Walden made a

real contribution to Antarctic sledging methods when he supplanted this rope with the G-pole, which he had learned to use in Alaska. As will be seen from the photographs the G-pole is a sturdy stick about six feet long, which is securely lashed to the forward end of one of the runners and cross-pieces and elevated at the free end. When the sledges needed any attention, we used to hang onto the G-pole with one hand, and push along beside the sledge with a ski stick in the other. It was easy to guide the sledges in this way and if it were necessary to make a quick stop the whole sledge could be swung around cross-wise to the trail by using the G-pole for a lever.

At least three different types of dog harnesses were tried out and we found that the leather collar style was the best. This harness is similar in all its essentials to the kind of harness used on draft horses. On the Greenland side of Arctic America it is commonest practice to hitch each dog on the end of a line several feet long which is attached directly to the sledge. The various lines radiate from the front of the sledge so that when travelling along in good order, the dogs are spread out fan wise. A great advantage of this style is that if one dog falls through the ice or gets into difficulty, he does not pull the whole team with him. But it is not the most efficient way to make use of all the dog power. On the other side of Arctic America, in Alaska, when the snow is deep the dogs are frequently hitched in tandem — in a long string with one dog immediately behind another. But where the snow is not too deep and where every bit of dog pulling power is important, the best arrangement seems to be to have the dogs hitched in pairs on opposite sides of a long rope or gangline which is attached to the sledge. Attached to the front end of this gangline, and therefore ahead of all the rest, is the lead dog. Jack Bursey, who had spent much of his early years in Newfoundland driving dogs with the Greenland or fan hitch, tried it out in the Antarctic but promptly gave it up for this method of driving the dogs in pairs.

A most important point about caring for the dogs comes from the problem of what to do with them at night. We never found it safe to let them run loose. They had to be staked out in such fashion that they could neither get free themselves, nor reach any of their neighbors, nor get too badly tangled. From the aviation supplies we procured several lengths of light steel control cables such as were used on the big Ford plane. Loops were spliced into each end so the cables could be securely staked to the ground and then Benny Roth fastened short lengths of chain at regular intervals along these cables. These chains were long enough to allow the dogs to turn around as many times as they saw fit before they settled themselves for the night, but were also short enough to prevent them from stealing their neighbors' food, or engaging them in quarrels on any other grounds.

A number of tests demonstrated that for the kind of burners we expected to use, commercial gasoline was the most efficient fuel. We escaped the trouble which so many sledgers have had from leaky oil cans, for Tom Mulroy reinforced all the cans we expected to use and packed them so securely that we never had to give them a thought. Not once did we have to mend a leak and we never lost any fuel due to faulty containers.

Since fuel was a fairly heavy item in our supplies, it is at once evident that every means should be taken to see that it was used economically. The efficiency of the fuel is directly dependent upon the cooking arrangements. Though many devices have been tried, it has yet to be demonstrated that there is any more reliable and efficient type of burner for fuels in cold regions than the well-known primus stove. Our cooker was built around a two-burner primus stove and was constructed entirely in Little America by Victor Czegka. It was designed by him after the principle which Fridtjof Nansen had found so successful and efficient. We therefore called it the Nansen-Czegka Cooker.

It will be clear from the diagram just how the cooker operated. I don't believe a more efficient and a more handy arrangement has been devised for the kind of cooking that we had to do. Obviously the snow in the central pot melts long before that in the ring and top pots but only a small amount of water is formed from this original melting. Not enough to make our "hoosh." To avoid the task of taking the cooker apart to refill this pot with snow, and thus allow a considerable loss of heat, Czegka placed spigots in both the ring and top pots which made it an easy matter to draw the water off these pots and pour it down the funnel through the top pot into the central one. When the water in this pot began to boil the top pot was removed and the ingredients of our prospective hoosh were dumped in. It was ready to eat within three to five minutes. An extra pot identical with this central one was then filled with water and placed over the flames. The water in this pot became hot as we ate our stew and when it came to a boil we brewed our tea. Now as we drank our tea the emptied hoosh pot which had been filled with water was getting hot to cook the oatmeal. This water came to a boil about the time we were finishing our supper; the oatmeal was dumped in and just allowed to come to a boil when it was poured into the vacuum jug.

Our eating gear consisted of one aluminum bowl, one enameled cup, and one wooden spoon each. The wooden spoon was a good tool, for if one used a metal spoon when it was very cold and should absent-mindedly stick it into his mouth without having first immersed it in the hot hoosh, he might well-nigh turn his mouth inside out.

Navigation of the party was my own special interest. I took both a theodolite and a sextant and 4 watches with stop watch, for making astronomical observations. After trying a number of compasses we found that a small boat compass was about the only type that would remain anywhere near steady when mounted on a sledge. When one is travelling on a meridian, that is north or south, he can keep an accurate check on his course during clear weather with a sun compass, but going east or west, crossing meridians, the sun compass becomes impracticable. Though we steered always with the magnetic boat compass we checked it at frequent intervals with the sun compass. This was important for the magnetic lines of force were weak and not only did the compass dial wobble a great deal but the variation was found to actually change in one place as much as two degrees within a single day. We had two sledge meters, made from bicycle wheels, which Amundsen had sent over from Norway, for keeping our distances by dead reckoning. One of these he had used himself on an Arctic Expedition and the name of his ship — the Maud — was stamped on the side.

One follows much the same procedure navigating on land as he does at sea, but of course can do it much more accurately in the former case. Though time in itself is not an essential factor in deciding on the most advantageous method, yet when the weather is so cold that it is misery to manipulate pencils and charts, short cuts and short methods are most welcome. Because all of the necessary tables for its use are so light and compact, and because it is short and was accurate within my needs, I used Weems' Tables for Line of Position throughout the sledge journey.

For our further projected work we carried 4 aneroid barometers including a very accurate surveying type which was to be used as a standard, 1 prismatic compass for each man, 1 large geologist's compass for use on jacob staff, 1 pocket compass and transit, 3 carefully tested thermometers, binoculars, notebooks, charts, tables, and the necessary scales, etc.

Since the caches of food and fuel deposited in the depots on our way south were to sustain us on the return journey, it was most necessary that we be able to relocate them easily. We therefore planned to mark the main trail with flags spaced a half mile apart. Then to the east and west of the depots, that is to the right and left of the main trail, we planned to place a row of these flags five miles out and spaced only a quarter of a mile apart. These side flags were to have their sticks or supports marked serially, beginning with one and proceeding away from the depot in either direction. Flags to the east were to be marked with an E together with the appropriate number while those to the west would be marked with a W. Thus a flag stick with W-8 on it would be eight flags, or two miles west of the depot. We reasoned that if we lost the main trail we might stumble onto one of the side flags, and with it so marked, would know at once just how to proceed to find the depot. We further planned to safeguard our homeward trek by placing large flags on the tops of the big snow beacons that we built around our caches of supplies or depots, and then at every noonday and night stop that did not coincide with a depot location we planned to build high snow beacons topped with flags. Experimentation had demonstrated that sort of an orange color showed up against the snow much better than any other color — much better for instance than black or red. Accordingly the material for our flags was made of a tough non-fading cotton fabric of such a color.

Just how to manage the great number of flags we needed to carry out such a comprehensive system of marking, and still not add an altogether impossibly heavy weight to our loads, was a problem. The rigid wooden sticks which had been used during the first summer by the southern sledging party under Vaughan were entirely too heavy and too bulky. I think it was our resourceful " boy scout man," Paul Siple, who gave us the solution to the problem. It was to use small pieces or splinters of bamboo made by splitting up the large stalks we had. Our flags were only about 10 by 14 inches in size and did not need very sturdy supports. We found that a sliver no larger than one's little finger proved to be ample support and had the further advantage of withstanding more wind than the rigid stick. The bamboo splinter was so pliable that the wind might blow hard enough to bend it over until it looked like a croquet arch, yet when the wind ceased it righted itself.

The very greatest departure made in our equipment and plans from other sledging parties was the inclusion of the radio. Others under similar conditions had always been cut off from their base from the time of their departure until their return. Mason and Hanson had designed sets for our use on the trail that for durability and simplicity of operation have not been surpassed. Since our coöperation with the polar flight plans depended upon the success of our radio communication and since our failure to make contact with Little America over any considerable length of time would necessarily occasion alarm there, it was necessary that we make plans as to what we should do in such an event. Freddy Crockett had made such admirable progress in mastering the work of operating the radio, that I anticipated no trouble from his end — nor did we ever have any. But there was always the possibility that the radio might get broken beyond repair from the heavy handling to which we had to subject it; and of course it might fall into a crevasse.

We knew that failure in our communications would cause Commander Byrd to fly out to see what the trouble might be.

With the help of Harold June and Dean Smith, the following set of signals were devised to enable us to make known our wishes to a plane flying over us. These designs were made by arranging three strips of orange cloth, 15 feet long by one and a half feet wide, flat on the snow as indicated in the diagrams.

1. Good field — land in neighborhood of T and in direction which it points.
2. Fair field — landing should be all right if done carefully. Put skis down as close as possible to the T.
3. Dangerous to land — unsuitable except in case of grave emergency.
4. Impossible to land.
5. Wait for further signals — as for instance putting out T in some place a little distance from where signalling is being done.

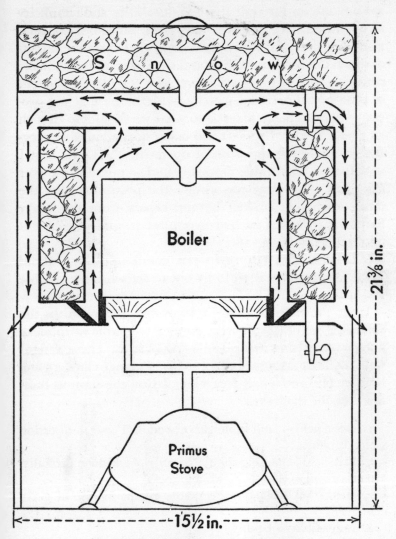

THE NANSEN-CZEGKA COOKER

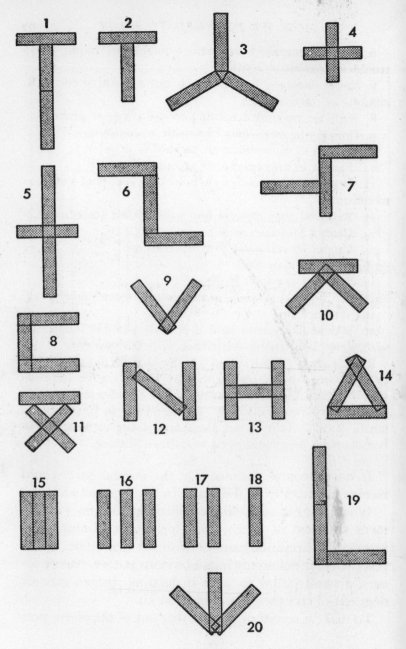

SIGNAL PATTERNS AS DESCRIBED ON PAGES 96 AND 97

6. We do not need assistance — unable to locate radio trouble — anxious to continue.

7. Radio damaged beyond repair but everything else O.K. anxious to continue.

8. Shall we proceed according to pre-arranged plans?

9. Dogs giving out — may be unable to continue.

10. Forced to discontinue on account of dogs.

11. Forced to discontinue on account of men.

12. Dog food unsatisfactory — must have supply of seal meat to continue.

13. Received your message and will proceed accordingly.

14. Cannot find message — please repeat.

15. Unable to carry out your instructions.

16. We need man food.

17. We need dog food.

18. We need immediate assistance — personnel emergency.

19. We need fuel.

20. Would like you to land if possible without interfering with your plans. Desire conference with Commander.

Plane signals " Understand " by making small " s " — indicates intention to land by figure " 8." Desire further information by signals by circling more than once. A dip and on with plane means everything O.K. Jazzing motor in near vicinity means poor visibility from plane and desire to have smoke bombs set off by ground party to assist in landing.

It was of course assumed that the ground party could receive messages from the plane by message parachute.

What might be considered our further emergency equipment consisted of Alpine rope for use in climbing and negotiating crevassed regions with greater safety, crampons where the climbing might be steep and icy, Alpine ice axes, a small pulley to assist in hauling sledges, men or dogs out of crevasses, and a medical kit.

To make a record of the carrying out of the above program we carried what we thought would be an adequate amount of both still and motion picture film and the necessary cameras for using it.

With all of our equipment gathered together we found the total weights to be:

	lbs.	oz.
Personal equipment	449	2
Man food	1228	
Cam gear and fuel	331	5
Dog food	2674	
Dog equipment	58	
Extra or spare sledge supplies	12	4
Instruments, navigating, etc.	91	
Trail markers	173	10
Motion picture equipment	65	2
Still camera supplies	18	5
Radio outfit complete	300	
Alpine ropes, etc.	40	
Tools	20	
Total	5489	
Load per team	1097	

It seemed to us that we had cut our weights down wherever we possibly could and yet this total was staggering. Our teams were light and a load of 8 to 9 hundred pounds at most was all that we should have expected them to carry. We didn't see where we could cut our loads down and quite blindly went ahead assuming that we could carry out the project in all its details.

We carefully planned the distribution of our supplies and equipment in the various sledge loads, so that with the exception of radio, we did not have all of our eggs in one basket. We even carried an extra cooker of simple design, so that two of our sledge outfits were completely self sustaining and except for cookers so were the other three. But in the face of a dire emergency that might have lost both cookers, we could doubtless have gotten along and satisfied our thirst for some time by judiciously eating snow.

In addition to all of the above weights that we hoped to handle, it was further planned that the supporting party would distribute dog food for us as follows:

```
Leave at depot number 1 . . . . . .  180 lbs.
   "     "     "      "    2 . . . . . ,  180  "
   "     "     "      "    3 . . . . . .  195  "
   "     "     "      "    4 . . . . . .  603  "
Total . . . . . . . . . . . . . . . . . . . . .  1158 lbs.
```

They were to leave Little America with 378 pounds of this dog food and pick up the rest from the caches left during the first summer's trip at the 20 mile, the 41 mile and the 46 mile stations south of Little America.

CHAPTER IV

SPRING

The morn is up again, . . .
And living as if earth contained no tomb,
And glowing into day: we may resume
The march of our existence.

And thou, the bright eye of the universe
That openest over all, and unto all
Art a delight.

BYRON

THOUGH we had scarcely noticed the disappearance of the sun on the 19th of April, we were a bit eager for his return. On each clear day at noon in the early part of August, the northern sky was so bright that it seemed as if the sun must surely pop up above the horizon any minute. In this way we were led up to the climax of its ultimate return on the 22nd of August.

During the latter days of August and the early part of September we had a sort of repetition of the long colorful twilight days of late March and early April. As we watched the miracle of the returning sun we could easily understand how man might worship him, purely from the standpoint of beauty. The color effects seemed to have been cumulative. It was as though the sun had been storing up over the four months that he had been gone for the great splashes that colored the early days of his return. And it

ROUGH SLEDGING THROUGH PRESSURE RIDGE
ON BAY OF WHALES

PRESSURE ROLL OR ANTICLINE OF ICE
ON BAY OF WHALES

is when the sun is near the horizon that the snow takes on its richest colorings, shading from the pale blue of celestite to the deepest purples where the shadows are heaviest. It is a kind of giant fairyland for in the flatly oblique rays of the sun everything casts long skeletal shadows that give an effect of only semi-reality.

We were glad to have the sun back for it meant the beginning of the fruition of the plans over which we had toiled throughout the weeks of the long night, and we were glad too, for there were some who needed the activity that the daylight meant. Ours was in general a goodly company yet there were bound to be some in so large a one, who had not found the long night as satisfying as had many others.

One does not need to have spent a winter in the Antarctic to realize that 42 men living in a society much more compact than that of an ordinary family, are bound to come to know each other very well; too well in some cases. The closer people are brought together the greater possibility there is of friction. We had been better off with a company not so large for we had too many men for our accommodations. We found the veneer of civilization to be rather thin in some cases; it was easily rubbed off and what was revealed was not always pleasant. Whatever there was of falseness as well as of fineness in a man's nature was bound to be revealed. Curiously enough irritability and " crabbiness " were not the most offensive personal traits; indeed I think one of the brightest and most refreshing men among us was one who fairly bristled at times with these qualities and fairly prided himself on them. Once in a moment of specially great irritation he declared that there were just 41 men in Little America against him! The one quality in a man's character that was most necessary and transcended all the rest was of course honesty. In no company was frankness such a necessary part of one's attitude; the unforgivable sin was duplicity.

But those more unfortunate qualities never loomed large among us. As time passed men of character and poise unconsciously added an increasingly individual effect which made the picture of the whole, a colorful and interesting mosaic of personality. In such a life it matters little whether a man is a corporal or a captain, the strong man will dominate.

As I think back upon it all now, the one thing that stands out most vividly, is the realization that a man's ability to stand the strain of such intimate living with his fellow men is generally fairly well proportionate to his inner resources. It was the men of mental resources, men with backgrounds of culture and education who best kept their poise. Even so I think a good deal of humbug exists in the minds of people who have never spent a night in the polar regions about the " terrible monotony " of the long continued darkness. I think such monotony as existed among us was derived from the fact that we got tired of each other; I never heard anyone in any way link any feeling of depression he might have had with the darkness. And after all why should any man of even reasonable education, with all his bodily comforts adequately cared for, find himself growing stale or glum when he has at his disposal a fairly comprehensive library of some 3000 volumes, to say nothing of the other factors that contributed to keep us all healthy and sane?

With its changing character and colorful variety I can see no good reason why the night should pall on any man's feelings; but then of course it all depends on one's point of view. If one wills it to be always bleak and unfriendly he can find the Antarctic eminently so, but if he is so minded, he can equally well find it satisfying and full of charm and glamour, and for him who knows how to grasp it, there is high adventure too.

Even though the returning sun seemed to have brought no heat with it, it was nevertheless the signal for us to begin active preparations for the second season's work. We began to emerge from our ground-hog-like existence of the preceding four months and to take on the normal activities of an outdoor community.

Commander Byrd was exceedingly anxious to have the geological party reach the Queen Maud Mountains before the polar flight was made, and of course we were no less anxious to get there with all possible speed for we wanted all the time we could possibly have in the field. Consequently we concentrated a great deal of attention on the dogs, for they had been idle all winter and would need considerable training before they would be fit for the trail. The first activity to be restored to the out-of-doors was therefore that concerned with the dogs. Early in September, in spite of the intense cold, the dog drivers began digging the crates out of the tunnel walls and placing them on the surface so that the dogs would be more easily available. And not only did the old dogs need a good deal of training, but the pups we expected to use had to be broken in. Withal, these early spring days were extremely busy ones for the dog drivers.

Balchen was not far behind with the aviation end of the expedition. Even as the dog crates began to make their appearance on top of the surface, he was at work with his gang digging out the planes and getting them ready to fly. The Fairchild was completely out and in readiness to take off before any of the dog teams started southward, so that had anything happened to any of them it would have been a comparatively simple matter to have flown out to discover the trouble.

We were greatly hampered in all of our work by the persistently low temperatures. Though the sun was perceptibly higher each day the air did not seem to warm up at all. September was the only month in the whole year that the temperature never once got up as high as zero. There were frequent stretches when it was well below *minus 60* degrees and the average for the whole month was 10 degrees lower than had been the average for Amundsen's September back in 1911, within three miles of Little America.

The daylight hours seemed to lengthen by leaps and bounds; on September 25th I find the following entry in my diary:

" The day's work is done but darkness fills only a part of the sky now, and it is no longer an opaque darkness, for when there are no clouds a pink glow follows the southern rim of our world throughout the night. Not long now until we shall have a midnight sun and then light, light, light — brilliant, blinding, dazzling light for weeks and months on end." To me the bright light of the all day summer became more monotonous than was the darkness of the long night.

September ended in a fairly furious blizzard. We took this as a good sign that the weather was beginning to break up for the spring. But it was not so, for October came in cold, very cold. This was most discouraging for we wanted to get the supporting party started on its way in the very

earliest part of this month. In anticipation of their departure we thought it wise to make some reconnaissance
trips to locate the best trail across the Bay of Whales, and
on October 3rd, my diary contains the following account
of such a trip.

" To-day I drove down to the south end of the Bay of
Whales with Norman Vaughan to see whether we could
get up on to the shelf ice from there when once we started
south. We found a place where we shall be able to do it
rather easily.

" Some days ago I shaved my beard, believing it wise to
do so before starting on the trail. It was quite a change for
I had not shaved since leaving New Zealand. My face had
not gotten fully used to the change for I froze it time after
time to-day and in my photographic zeal I again froze the
fingers of my right hand. I must be careful there, for that
is getting to be too much of a habit. And now to-night
my face feels as though it had been sunburned and my
fingers feel as though they had been ground off with sand-
paper. My eyes smart too for my eyelids were often frozen
shut to-day. I am not sure but that I shall find it advisable
to cut my eyelashes shorter for my eyes water so much in
the cold that frequently to-day when I closed them, tears
would start to trickle out between the lashes and quickly
turn into little beads of ice that quite froze my eyes shut.

" The temperature hovered around 40 degrees below
zero all day and though I had only a windproof parka over
my woolen shirt I was fairly warm except for my face and
hands."

I should perhaps insert here that in the course of our
experience on the trail, we learned that freezing one's
face was not necessarily a serious matter. We kept watch

on each other and when a white spot indicating a frostbitten condition appeared, one usually needed but to hold his hand over it for a few seconds to restore the circulation. Ofttimes when we were sledging along and our bodies were very warm we produced the same effect by simply pulling the parka hood around so as to cut off the wind. One might suffer parts of his face to be frostbitten several times in a day without ill effect if he took care of it promptly. If the freezing is allowed to continue through to the bone the consequences are apt to be serious.

Naturally we had learned from Stefansson that the sane thing to do when we were frostbitten was simply to warm up the affected part — never, never to accentuate the condition by rubbing snow on it. When I came into the mess hall from the day's trip described by the above entry from my diary, one of the men exclaimed,

" Why, Larry — your face is frozen! "

I looked into a mirror and found that both cheeks and chin were quite white with frostbites. I did the unorthodox thing of standing by the stove while my face thawed out and the only after effects were as noted above, such burning effect as one might notice after a sunburn.

Cold or no cold, preparations went steadily on and we tentatively set Monday October 7th as the day for the supporting party to start south. We had further decided to leave at the same time with the teams of the geological party and accompany the supporting party for two or three days. We expected that we could in this way get an idea of how they were going to get along and would at the same time have an opportunity to check up on the performance of our own equipment.

We began loading our sledges on Sunday for the projected start on the next day. When Freddy Crockett and Norman Vaughan had finished putting the supplies into the canvas tanks on their sledges and started to lash them up, they found that they could not pull on the canvas without tearing it apart. Thinking to make the sledges more conspicuous against the snow, we had dyed the canvas tanks with orange colored dye and now to our great distress we learned that the dye had rotted the canvas. It was evident that new tanks would be necessary before we could finally get under way. Both Martin Ronne and Alexander were pressed into service to make them for us.

With the failure of our canvas tanks on our hands, it would have been impossible for us to have started out on the following morning with the supporting party, but as it turned out this did not matter for Monday the 7th was impossibly cold and so it continued throughout the week. Badly as we all wanted to get into the field, we knew that if we wore our dogs out at the very start there would be no hope of ever seeing the Queen Maud Mountains, for we had no reserve dogs to draw upon. We had to be careful for not only is it much harder for the dogs themselves to stand heavy work when the temperature is very low but the sledges pull much harder.

My physicist friends tell me that when a sledge is pulled across the snow under good sledging conditions, the friction of the runners on the snow causes an infinitesimal amount of melting so that the sledge really glides along on a thin film of water. If the temperature is too low, not enough friction is developed to cause such melting and the sledge drags in the hard crystals of the snow quite as though it were being pulled through sand. On the other hand if the temperature is too high, too much melting may result and little beads of ice may freeze onto the wooden runners; these hold the sledge back a great deal; of course if the temperature gets so high that the snow is actually sticky, wooden runners are quite impracticable and must be sheathed with some such metal as steel. We did not need to worry about such high temperatures on our proposed journey and of course did not take any metal shoes for our wooden runners. We found that the best sledging temperatures for our wooden runner sledges ranged from about 15 to 20 degrees above zero; but the temperature might fall as low as 20 degrees below zero without the additional burden being greatly noticed by the dogs. However when the temperature got down into the minus forties the surface became one of sand. The very worst temperatures were over 25 degrees above zero when the snow began to get sticky.

We delayed starting from Little America hoping to have temperatures of at least 20 degrees below zero for the supporting party to begin its trip.

Our enforced stay in Little America beyond the date we had set for departure made the time lag a bit, but it gave me opportunity to investigate further some local ice phenomena to see what changes had taken place over the winter.

The various forms which the ice of the Bay of Whales assumed under the stress of the great lateral pressures to which it was subjected, had always been a source of greatest interest to me, for the structures that resulted were identical with those formed when rocks are under similar stresses. Only such changes take place in the rocks over periods of time far too long to be actually observed by man, but here in the Bay of Whales, over a period of but a few weeks one might see the various structures of folded mountains actually forming. Anticlines, synclines and all kinds of faults were formed almost under one's eyes; it was a geological study of unparalleled interest to me.

Davies and I were furthermore interested in the formation of crevasses and their associated phenomena about the Bay of Whales, and particularly in that portion of the shelf ice upon which Little America had been built. For our village was located in a little basin only 30 feet above sea level which was surrounded on three sides by higher, older areas of shelf ice. According to Martin Ronne, who was with Amundsen when the latter was establishing his winter quarters at Framheim, the Little America basin was then a bay of open water with an iceberg in it. In most places where this basin of ours merged with the higher shelf ice about it there were to be found crevasses, or in lieu of them, definitely aligned " haycocks." With the help of Arnold Clark, who manipulated the ropes, Taffy Davies and I used to descend into the crevasses to study the temperature conditions and the ice crystals that lined the walls of many of them.

One day Dr. Coman and I had been following along the margin of the basin, studying the haycocks and taking some pictures of them, and were headed back toward the camp when suddenly the surface gave way under one of Dana's feet; he had stepped onto the thin roof of a crevasse that gave no surface indication at all of its existence. We craned our necks to look down the hole thus made and beheld a fairy palace of such rare beauty that there was just nothing we could say about it. We had neither the time nor the equipment with us to investigate it then, but the very next day, Taffy, Arnold, and

I came over with ropes and ladders prepared to make a descent.

Getting down this crevasse proved to be relatively easy, for it was only from three to ten feet wide and not more than eighteen feet deep and at the bottom we found a floor of old sea ice where we could walk about with ease. It was some minutes before we could bring ourselves to the necessity of breaking off any of the crystals for study and for measurement, because the merest touch or even the brush of one's light parka against the wall sent a small glass-like avalanche shattering about one's feet. No Aladdin with his wonder lamp ever dreamed a crystal palace one half so lovely as this ice palace of ours. The walls were completely studded with an unthinkable maze of paper thin ice crystals of unbelievable fragility, and in places they hung in great masses from the roof like huge candelabra, and the thin snow cover let enough light filter through to give to the whole atmosphere just the right touch of unreality. The upper part of our fairy palace was filled with the palest blue light which darkened with depth into sapphire and at the bottom our feet were almost hidden in the ultramarine blue " darkness." Our faces took on a ghastly sort of pallor in this blue light.

In all of our observations and measurements made here and elsewhere, we never found two crystals alike, yet they were all devised after the same general pattern, that is they all belonged in the same hexagonal crystal system. It was a source of increasing wonder to us to note the intricate and fantastic shapes into which these crystals were formed so that they all followed the same general pattern but never duplicated a design. Individual crystals from five to ten inches across were common and they ranged from this size down to microscopic forms. Taffy was able to observe the growth of crystals over a long period of time and found that even slight changes in the temperature or the moisture content of the air caused almost endless variety in the crystals that were forming. He further learned that under ideal conditions crystals grew very fast and that one of our crystal palaces might have been built within a few weeks.

In properly sheltered places we found another development of crystals known as frost flowers or ice flowers. It appears that when a pool of sea water freezes over quickly, particles of salt separate out on top of the ice. If humid air happens to be blown across this new ice, the moisture, from the air, crystallizes around the salt particles as nuclei, in little bouquets that look like feathery fern-like fronds of the most delicate lace. Individual bouquets may be as much as four or five inches high and I have never seen anything that gave an impression of such complete fragility as did these. Just a whisper of a breeze and they were shattered into a million pieces and strewn across the ice.

The term "haycock" is not entirely descriptive for the conical shaped mounds of ice and snow that we found in places along the margin of the Little America basin. These symmetrically shaped hills ranged in height from two to twenty feet and looked like nothing so much as gigantic blisters, and "blisters" I believe they essentially were. It is inconceivable that lateral pressures could be so equally distributed as to push up such mounds, nor could they have been formed primarily by the accumulation of drift snow about some solid object, such as another block of snow. They were too localized for any such method of formation and besides snow never drifts into such steep sided symmetrical piles as these. Furthermore

we found that the tops of these mounds were always fractured in such a manner as to force one to conclude that
the force causing the fracturing had come from within.
Often their tops looked like the thin crust of new earth
just being broken by a bean or pea pushing its way upward, but on an infinitely larger scale of course. Often the
fractured tops had been healed by snow or ice, but where
they were open, rising currents of air were actively de-
positing ice crystals around the rims of the openings; such
a method of building may account for a portion of the
growth of these structures but it was very evidently not
the primary one. The only feasible explanation of their
origin seemed to be that it was due primarily to some force
pushing up from below; gas bodies or air under great
pressure beneath the ice might cause just such structures
to start at least, and Wright and Priestly [1] indicate that
there is definite evidence of the occurrence of such gas
bodies under the ice.

We decided that a study of the interior of one of these
" haycocks " would throw a conclusive light upon the
question of its origin. If they were formed from some in-
ternal force such as a gas under pressure, as I believed,
they ought to be at least partially hollow. Tom Mulroy
volunteered to blow one up with dynamite. After several
attempts he made a very successful shot which blew the
top and part of a side off one, and though the structure
had a snow-ice rind from a few inches to as much as five
feet in thickness, there was a cave or grotto underneath.
This grotto was lined with ice crystals in quite the same
fashion that many of the crevasses were.

[1] C. S. Wright and R. E. Priestly. Glaciology (British (Terra Nova) Antarctic Expedition, 1910–1913), London, 1922, pp. 343–344.

Saturday morning, October 12th, we awoke to find a typical Antarctic blizzard raging out of doors, and again we hoped that it meant a change for warmer weather. But the decided rise in temperature that usually accompanied high winds did not come with this one. Several men froze parts of their faces just walking the two hundred yards from the Administration Building to the mess hall for breakfast. Our October was being just as much colder than Amundsen's had been as had our September been colder than that he recorded near by. When he finally left Framheim on October 19th for his journey to the South Pole, the temperature was 1 degree above zero and his coldest for the whole month was 20 degrees below zero; so far as the latter had been nearer our warmest than our coldest.

Sunday the 13th was bright and fair but still bitterly cold. It did not seem wise to make the final start yet, but since one of the hardest parts of the trip would be getting across the Bay of Whales with its immense pressure ridges, and up onto the shelf ice at the south end of the bay, we decided to have both the supporting party and the geological party cross the bay with their front sledges on this Sunday. This would give us a good start for the real take-off.

All of the teams of both parties, except Jack O'Brien's, went on this preliminary trip. The whole round trip was not more than 14 to 16 miles but the dogs came back very tired. Mike Thorne insisted that the loads were far too heavy and that we had either to lighten them or to wait for much warmer weather. We still lived in hopes of having warmer weather.

Monday was still too cold for the final departure, but

I decided to drive across the bay with O'Brien who planned to take his front sledge over so that he would not be handicapped at the time when all of the teams left. The dogs were in good shape and worked splendidly, but it was disquieting to see the difficulty with which they handled this single sledge.

The uncertainty of the weather was growing harder to stand than the uncertainty of being able to sledge under such adverse temperature conditions, and accordingly Tuesday morning October 15th both parties started south. Carl Peterson accompanied the supporting party to help Joe de Ganahl with his radio and Joe Rucker went with the geological party to get some motion pictures of both parties together; Commander Byrd and a goodly number of others from Little America came along to the end of the bay to see us off.

It was a discouraging day. Without exception our loads were excessive and none of the teams were hauling the heaviest loads that our plans called for. Mike had been right. It was expected that the supporting party would pick up additional supplies at the 20 mile station established the previous fall, and we knew that we should have to take on 600 pounds additional load when we reached the southward limit of the supporting party's trek at depot number 2. But very surely the dismal truth forced itself upon us that we could not carry out our projected plans with the dog power at our disposal. When we came to a slight rise in the snow surface no more than three to five inches high, we had to push on the sledges to help the dogs drag them over. Of course the temperature was 30 degrees below zero and we knew that the same loads would pull much more easily when it grew warmer. But we could not by any means bank upon the temperature as a determining factor in our success.

We had advanced our complete loads, that is the two sledges in tandem, only 8 miles beyond the place where we had picked up our heavy or front sledges at the head of the Bay of Whales, when we had to stop and make camp out of consideration for the dogs. It was a gloomy night. We put up our tents, staked out the dogs and fed them, and soon they rolled themselves into balls to keep warm and were fast asleep. While the drivers were attending to the needs of the dogs, I was busy with supper. The cooker worked inordinately slowly; it took three times as long to melt snow as it had in the various tests we had made with it back in Little America and it had grown late before we finished with our evening hoosh. I gave my place in the tent with O'Brien and Thorne to Joe Rucker and planned to spend my night in the cook tent. It was cold when I wriggled myself part way down into my sleeping bag and sat up to write the account of the day in my log book. The sky was overcast and the light was quite dim by this time. I wrote several lines and then held the book up close to my eyes to look at it, only to find that the page was still blank. I found that my pencil was all right and then I discovered that as I had held the book close to my face to write, the moisture from my breath had condensed in the form of a thin film of ice on the paper and my pencil had just glided across it without making any impression. It was 30 degrees below zero in my tent as I sat there writing.

My ideal sleeping bag didn't seem so ideal in practice. I shivered all night. I think it is an illusion that one is necessarily adapted to things that he especially likes to do. There are few things that I should like so much to do as sing, and yet nobody has ever yet been kind enough to tell me that I had even the slightest aptitude for it; likewise I had never in all my life wanted to do anything quite so much as I wanted to make this sledge trip, but I got cold very easily. It seemed much more difficult for me to keep warm than it was for anyone else in the party.

From their experience on the trail during the first season, Crockett, Thorne, Vaughan, and Goodale had learned that it was most efficient, when breaking a new trail with dog teams, to have a man ski out in front. The lead team followed him and thus a straighter course was kept. But it was necessary for this front man to have some guidance, so we planned to mount a boat compass on the front sledge and have someone ski alongside it to check the course, and call out to the man in front, as necessity demanded: " Right," " Left," or " Steady." Just by way of practice we decided to try out this method when we started out on the second morning, even though the supporting party would be ahead of us and we should not really be breaking a new trail. Mike Thorne was by far the best man of us all on skis and we had long since decided that he would be the logical one to have out in front. Since I was the navigator of the party, I planned to ski along beside Mike's sledge, driving his team and watching the compass at the same time.

I had never taken the trouble to practice driving a dog team on skis but it looked easy. I was sure I could hang onto the G-pole and manage the team with but little difficulty. But I had not reckoned on the undisciplined energy with which the dogs would be ready to start this second

A " Lodging for the Night "

day. I slid up beside Mike's front sledge on my skis and had just grabbed onto the G-pole when without waiting for my word of command, the dogs decided that it was time to start. I cannot quite understand yet how it all happened, but they turned and not only ran over me themselves, but pulled the front sledge with its heavy load across my arms, and then the rear sledge with its lighter load across my legs. There was a hard crust on the snow so I was well bruised. I pulled myself together and decided to let Mike drive his team until I got just a little bit more accustomed to skiing with a G-pole in one hand and a ski stick in the other.

The sledges dragged so heavily that the dogs' surplus energy had soon worn off. Within an hour I was able to ski alongside the sledge quite easily and when we came to the merest rise in the snow, I had to help the team with the sledge by giving the G-pole a jerk.

It was a gloomy sort of day. The supporting party had had even greater difficulty than had we and it was only by relaying a bit that we were all able to reach the 20 mile station. The outlook was depressing for it was evident that not only could the supporting party not take on the additional loads here as we had planned, but that their present loads should be lightened.

When the geological party left Little America we had planned to go south for only 2 days and then return to camp. We reasoned that we could then spend a few days correcting whatever deficiencies we had found in our equipment, before taking our final leave. When we established radio communication with Little America that night I sent a rather dismal report back to Commander Byrd and informed him that according to plans we would return to Little America the next morning. He thought this unwise and urged us to carry on a few days more with the supporting party.

There were two reasons why I thought this was not feasible; first our cooker had almost completely failed to work for there was a big leak in it somewhere that I had been unable to locate, and could not have mended in any case; secondly, it was apparent to all of us that there was not the slightest possibility of carrying out our original plans entirely with the dogs, and we hoped that when Commander Byrd understood the situation he would see his way clear to having the Fairchild plane help us out, at least one or two hundred miles with part of our too heavy loads. This was of course the chief reason why I took my geological party back to Little America the next morning. Carl Peterson and Joe Rucker came back with us.

We talked the whole matter over with the Commander but failed to convince him that it was advisable to risk either of the planes for the purpose of helping us to lay our bases of supplies. We then had to face the necessity of curtailing our original plans. We gave up our plans and hopes of reaching the mountains before the polar flight was made, and therefore abandoned the idea of taking a radio direction finder to assist the polar party in locating the mountain base, which we had hoped to establish for them.

We had expected to let the supporting party get about a week's start ahead of us, but now instead of doing this, we decided to take Commander Byrd's suggestion and have the five teams of the geological party depart at once and move as much of our big loads as possible out to depot number 2, and then return to Little America for a last brief rest and overhauling before the final start. Since the party was to proceed over a well marked trail and was to return by the same route, there was no reason for me to go along. I should have been so much dead weight since I would not have been driving a team myself. Furthermore Dr. Coman was rather insistent that I take things rather easily until I had somewhat recovered from the bruises I had sustained in my initial attempt to drive Mike's team. When he first looked me over Dr. Coman advised me that I had the worst case of " super-cubital ecchymosis " that he had ever seen, whereupon I was sure that I needed a rest!

It was a cold Sunday morning, October 25th, when my five companions started southward on their trip to depot number 2. Norman Vaughan was placed in charge of this so-called 100 mile (nautical miles) trip. I planned to spend the time while they were gone making such improvements in our equipment as had been suggested on our brief trip with the supporting party.

Without exception everyone in Little America was concerned over the fact that we might not be able to carry out our plans with sufficient completeness to give us time in the field to do the geological and geographical work we hoped to accomplish. Everyone wanted to help but aside from the airplanes, the only hope of assistance lay in the snowmobile. Jim Feury, who had driven it during the preceding fall was sure that it would work. Captain McKinley, who had some days before taken from my shoulders the responsibilities of the executive officer of the camp, now mustered all hands that could be of any assistance to Feury in getting the snowmobile dug out and in commission for the trail. On Monday the 21st it came out of its snow garage and on that date I find the following entry in my diary:

"I am still doubtful as to its possible usefulness in helping us on our way. Motor vehicles have never worked very successfully in polar exploration and I do not believe our present Ford snowmobile has the problem solved. Its performance last fall left much to be desired. Furthermore in order to help our sledging party now, it would have to go so far south as to make it expensive, just getting to the starting point where our heavy loads are."

But I knew full well that if the snowmobile failed to make good, that it would be through no fault of those who were so wholeheartedly getting it ready and who hoped to operate it. And I was like a drowning man grasping for a straw, for Norman was sending back disquieting reports about the condition of our dogs.

On the day my five companions departed they had easily reached the 20 mile station, where we had left our heavy loads, as we bade good-bye to the supporting party. On the 22nd and 23rd they had been obliged to travel against a wind from 15 to 20 miles an hour in velocity, with the temperature never above 20 degrees below zero. The drift was so bad that they had some difficulty seeing the flags that marked the trail. They made only 13 miles on Monday the 22nd and 16 on Tuesday. On Wednesday the outlook was so bad for the dogs that Norman sent me a message urging the return of the party from a point 75 miles south of Little America. He indicated that the dogs were weakening greatly in the low temperatures and that he thought this would be the best way to save them for the final journey. It was difficult for us back in Little

America to understand how we were going to be able to make as great a final journey as we had planned, if the teams could not at this time make the goal we had set, namely, depot number 2. I urged Norman to lighten the loads, to give the dogs a day of rest, to let the tired ones run loose — to do anything he thought necessary to make their goal without pushing the teams too hard. It was too early in the summer to lose any dogs and besides there was no emergency for letting them die from overwork.

They carried on making 14 miles on the 25th and then on the 26th by dint of travelling all day and up until 9 in the evening, they had reached depot number 2, 110 miles south of Little America. The temperature had been from 25 to 35 degrees below zero throughout this day and they had been able to travel the 27 miles only because they had, in the morning before they started, cached 750 pounds of dog food beside the trail.

From Norman's brief reports I gathered that the work was greatly lightened for the dogs when the flexible rawhide lashed sledges were used, for the same weight was hauled much more easily on such sledges than on the heavier rigid freight sledges. Norman advised me that if we had two more light trailer sledges we should be able to abandon at least one additional freight sledge and thus lighten the loads a little more for the dogs.

Though Strom was needed to assist with getting the snowmobile ready he dropped everything to make the needed sledges for us. He used old skis for runners and whatever else he could find about camp for the rest of the sledge structures. He worked night and day to finish them before he was needed to go with the snowmobile, and there is no doubt in my mind but that Strom's sledges were one of the very most important factors in the ultimate success of our trip.

Canvas tanks were necessary for the new sledges and with Strom-like zeal, Alexander forgot about sleep until he had them all finished.

In the meantime preparations for the departure of the snowmobile had been finished in feverish haste. One of the most difficult feats was that of getting it through and over the pressure ridges on the Bay of Whales. They had to cut roadways in many places, but it was finally across the bay and really on its way on Saturday the 26th. Strom was placed in charge and was navigator, Feury was engineer-driver and Black went along as his relief. They expected to pick up the heavy loads that the teams of my party had left at depot number 2 and haul them on to depot number 3, and perhaps out to the northern edge of the crevassed region between latitudes 81 and 82 degrees south.

Monday night, the 28th, my geological party returned. They were tired and the dogs were well-nigh worn out. This was not strange for they had made a hard trip and had come back the whole return distance of 110 miles in three days. They had met the snowmobile party 65 miles south of Little America and reported that it was humming along in great shape and that all three of the men who were manning it were in high spirits. This was most encouraging.

I was eager to get started southward again as promptly as possible, but there were so many details that had to be attended to that it was five days before we were finally ready.

Throughout all this time regular reports had been

coming back by de Ganahl's radio from the supporting party. Theirs had been a hard lot for they had not had the advantage of preliminary trips to test their equipment as had we; if they found anything wrong, they just had to put up with it. The weather had been bad and the temperatures consistently low throughout their journey, with the sledging of course proportionately hard for the dogs. They had found the crevassed region just as hazardous to cross as they had been led to believe it would be from Amundsen's accounts of it. But they had surmounted all obstacles and on November 1st had reached their goal — depot number 4 — 220 miles south of Little America.

CHAPTER V

SOUTHWARD

"The untold want, by life and land ne'er granted,
Now, voyager, sail thou forth to seek and find."

WALT WHITMAN

IT was a dull gray cheerless sort of day when we took our final departure from Little America on November 4th. But the day was somewhat in keeping with our spirits for the reports from the supporting party together with our own experiences on our two brief southward journeys did not combine to make us altogether sanguine as to the outcome of our efforts. The dogs were the great question. Ours was a nondescript collection, and though we were of necessity cutting down from our original schedule, we were still expecting almost super-dog things from them. Our preliminary trips had enabled us to find the flaws in our equipment. These had been corrected and we were as ready as we could ever hope to be, with the means at our disposal, for our final start.

We did not leave Little America until 1:30 but we had no loads to haul except our own personal gear and the camp equipment together with a little food, so we knew the dogs would have no difficulty in reaching our 20 mile station this first day. In fact the first 110 miles of our trip loomed easy for us since we should be able to ride all the way on our sledges.

There was no lack of whole-hearted sincerity with which everyone in Little America bade us good-bye and good luck. One of Commander Byrd's last requests was to give him any news we could pick up about the snowmobile party. We had had no word from them since they were seen by the geological party, homeward bound from the " 100 mile " trip. Things were going so merrily at that time that we were clinging to the hope that they had been able to reach depot number 2 and haul our heavy sledges fifty to seventy-five miles farther south. But we were all concerned over the prospect of their attempting to negotiate the crevasses between latitudes 81 and 82 with the snowmobile, and Commander Byrd had ordered the supporting party to leave instructions in a prominent place on the trail, ordering them not to attempt it. But there was always the possibility that they had not seen the orders and that they had found other crevasses that the dog teams had been able to cross in safety.

About 15 miles south of Little America out over the shelf ice ahead of us we saw a dark object for which we could not account. Now it looked like a canoe and again like a Zeppelin. We were almost upon it before we realized that it was the large khaki tent which the snowmobile party had taken with them. We surprised the members of the party inside it. They were unshaved and unwashed and had very evidently been working hard, for the snowmobile had broken down 85 miles south of Little America and they had already walked 70 miles of the distance back, hauling their tents, sleeping bags and food on a small sledge. We were sorry to know that the snowmobile had failed but were glad to find the party in such high spirits. They had done their best to help the work of the geological party along. The ideal mechanical vehicle for crossing the Antarctic snow and ice had not yet been invented. I am glad that it was not invented before we started on this sledge trip.

It was the loss of the plane in the blizzard over in the Rockefeller Mountains that made it necessary for me to go into the field this second summer with the dogs, and even though it might sound paradoxical, yet I am bound to say that I am glad circumstances opened the way for my participation in the sledging operations. So long as I live I shall be increasingly grateful for the fact that I was privileged to travel this long white road with the dogs. Like my friend, Knud Rasmussen, " From my heart I bless the fate that allowed me to be born at a time when Arctic exploration by dog sledge was not yet a thing of the past."

I think man has found no means of pioneering by land or sea or air, that reaches the high conception of polar sledging with dogs. I think no other method of travel can be as fascinating in its entirety and I know of no other activity that makes such complete demands on all that there is in a man. It demands the most rigid self-discipline or self-control; it calls for the utmost resourcefulness and it taxes the endurance of the hardiest. Nowhere else could there develop a more complete understanding between men, and if they be the right men, that means a finer understanding and appreciation of all that is most funda-mental in virile character. And here develops that friend-ship between man and his dogs which is second only to that between men. Only after one has followed them day after day and week after week, and seen them pull their lives out for him, with never a complaint, can he appreciate the devotion of which dogs are capable.

And so on November 4th began the high adventure of all the expedition for me — adventure and opportunity both — for I could not have been dropped any place in the world where I could have found so aptly combined and so perfectly balanced the glamour and romance of adventure with such rare opportunities for sound scientific research, for I was headed into a land of glaciers and ice clad mountains geologically and geographically untouched and unknown.

Beyond the 20 mile station the way was new for me, and, therefore, full of interest. As we headed south from this station we were sledging over an almost flat plain of snow, but by noon we began to climb a very gentle slope. When we stopped on the top of this rise our aneroid barometer indicated that we were 895 feet above sea level. Yet we were not on the highest part; we had but come to the top of the northern end of a great bulge or hill in the shelf ice, whose axis trended southeast to northwest and which we estimated to be at least fifty miles long. This hill got higher toward the southeast from us and we believe that at its greatest height it must reach an altitude of at least one thousand feet.

At 10:30 on the morning of this second day out from Little America we had arrived at depot number 1 where we took on two ice axes and a little food, but, of course, left the complete cache of dog food, man food, and fuel for our return journey.

As we came down off the hill we crossed a valley bounded in part by crevasses and haycocks. And ahead of us stretched an almost featureless plain of dead monotony as far as we could see. It proved to be just that for many miles.

On the morning of the seventh at 10:30 we met the homeward bound supporting party. They were all feeling fit but we could see that they had had a gruelling time throughout their trip. Their dogs seemed tired and worn and several had bleeding feet. Nevertheless, we selected two of Braathen's best ones in return for which we gave him our poorest one, and after listening carefully to their advice about crossing the crevassed regions we bade them good-bye and were on our way. Chris Braathen looked longingly after us. I wished that we might take him along, for there was no pose about his love for this kind of life. He didn't know there was such a word as hardship.

At noon of this same day we arrived at the deserted and forlorn looking snowmobile where we stopped for lunch. We added to our loads from here two ice axes, six pairs of crampons, and five gallons of gasoline, and left, as an emergency cache, twenty-five pounds of sugar, fifteen pounds of pemmican and ten pounds of biscuit.

I'm inclined to think that the next day, November 8th, was a day which is unique in polar sledging experience. If not unique in all sledging experience, it is yet unique in records of such. It was a gray morning of poor visibility and the dogs seemed more eager than ever to get started. The dogs are always restless for an hour or two in the morning, and this morning every team got into some sort of tangle before we finally got under way. I was riding with Eddie Goodale, and when we finally got his team untangled and started we could see no flags and of course, did not know just where the trail was. We, therefore, decided it would be wisest to retrace our steps until we came to the site of our camp and relocate the trail from there.

When we arrived back at our camp-site, I pulled out a pocket compass to see that we got started in the right direction.

"That is the way," I said, pointing as I thought due south.

The dogs were in fine fettle this morning and we slid along over the snow at a great rate. Shortly before noon we saw a high dark object dead ahead of us on the trail. We couldn't imagine what it was, but finally decided that it must be a sledge which the supporting party had abandoned and had stuck up on its end so that it would make a good marker for the trail. Satisfied with this explanation on we went, and we had actually come to within two hundred yards of it before we realized that the dark object was the snowmobile that we had passed at noon on the previous day! When we had left camp after having gotten off the trail in the morning I had directed my companions due north instead of south and the visibility had been so bad that none of us had sensed the fact that we were going back over the same trail that we had covered on the previous day.

It was now nearly noon and we had come back toward Little America nearly ten miles. There was nothing for us to do but stop and have lunch and then turn around. We had found it so easy to follow the trail marked by the supporting party ahead of us that I had not bothered to mount the boat compass on a non-magnetic sledge and I had checked the course this morning by just looking at a small pocket compass. Unfortunately both ends of the needle of this compass were almost alike. Furthermore,

the magnetic variation was here 114 degrees easterly. That
meant that we had to follow a course of *east northeast* by
compass to go due south geographically. But there were
really no extenuating circumstances for such a blunder.
Here was a day lost which I could charge to nothing but
my own carelessness — but if I needed a lesson now was
the time to have it. Needless to say, I mounted the boat
compass the next day and did not fail to keep check on the
course the rest of the summer, whether we were travelling
over a new trail or one that had been marked.

We found rough travelling on the 9th and went bouncing along over the rough sastrugi, but the loads were light
enough so that the dogs trotted along easily and brought
us to depot number 2 shortly after noon. Here we had
to begin our heavy work for this was the outpost reached
by my party on their preliminary trip; it was here that
they had left their heavily loaded front sledges. We spent
the afternoon repacking our sledges and building a high
beacon of snow blocks around our cache of supplies to be
left at this depot and then finished the day with our
Christmas dinner! George Tennant was so anxious that we
share the chicken dinner that he was already devising for
Christmas in Little America that he gave us a huge box
of chicken and vegetables to be cooked for our own dinner.
Much as we should have liked to carry this one normal
dinner to the mountains with us, we could not attempt
even this additional weight, so we cooked it as we went
about rearranging our sledges. It was a grand dinner and
we all appreciated George's thoughtfulness. Mike's and
OB's enjoyment was somewhat lessened on account of the
fact that they were suffering from snowblindness. Their
eyes were red and inflamed and, as Mike expressed it, felt

as though "someone had thrown hot sand into them."
One cannot be too careful about his eyes for even when
the clouds are thick and the light does not seem very
bright it is not safe to travel without colored glasses. But
when it is intensely cold it is a sore temptation to remove
the glasses, for in spite of every precaution one can take,
they are forever fogging up just from the moisture that
comes from one's breath. Of course, this moisture freezes
at once and one continually finds himself travelling
along trying to peer through glasses that are in very truth
" frosted."

Not until 10:30 on the morning of the 10th were we
ready to start with the real trials of the long pull ahead.
Each team was pulling at least 850 pounds and Freddy's
and OB's slightly more for they had to use the rigid
sledges in the lead. The rest were equipped with flexible
sledges throughout.

I think the dogs got on surprisingly well this day with
their heavy loads. I was so busy looking after myself and
keeping up with them that I had no time to give them
any attention and much less any sympathy. For as the
dogs had taken on their additional sledges here, we had
to take to our skis entirely as our means of getting along.
The sledge loads were far too heavy for us to think of
riding. I promptly learned how different a thing it was
to " putter " around on skis about Little America than
to keep at it steadily as I had to here. I shall never forget
this first day on skis. How many times I fell down and
in what curious positions I arrived on the snow could
scarcely be described. To add to my distress, as the day
wore on, my right ski boot began to chafe my heel. I was
glad to have Norman agree with me that we should not

try to drive the dogs far this first day with their heavy loads. Even so the 14 miles we covered had been about the hardest journey I had ever made in one day.

Had I known at the end of the first day how much harder the second would be, I think I would have been tempted to look around for a nice deep crevasse. Though the sun was bright there was a little breeze right in our faces and any kind of breeze when the temperature is 15 degrees below zero is nasty. The night's rest had not given my heel the relief I expected and my ski boots were as rigid as iron which did not help matters at all. Of course, my boots were lined with a layer of rime when I took them off at night but I never dreamed that mere leather could so nearly approach the physical characteristics of steel as my boots had done over night. Getting into one's ski boots any morning is one of the bitterest trials of the day but when one has to lever the boot over a blistered heel the trial is fraught with excruciating pain.

Never before or since have I ended a day in such complete and hopeless misery as I did this second day of independent travel on skis. Every stride of my right ski sent pains shooting up from my heel. I never would have believed that my legs could get so lame and sore without actually falling off. I reached the limit of my dejection when I began to count the flags along the way in the afternoon. I knew that the supporting party had placed these flags every half mile. I had told my companions that we would go 16 miles to-day and now I began to reckon the number of flags that we still had to pass. Then descending still lower in morale I counted the number of strides between two flags and began to count the number that I should still have to make.

Finally at the end of a day which had seemed years long, we stopped. When I took off my skis and started to help make camp, I found that my legs had become quite unmanageable. They did not always take me where I willed to go, and for the life of me I could not step over a three inch strip of canvas to get into the cook tent. I had to take my hands and lift each foot over and then follow them into the tent, as it were. I sat down to start the primus stove in the cooker and found myself so exhausted that I could scarcely keep awake. When I got so near asleep that I felt a bowl or spoon slipping from my fingers I would give my right foot a little jerk. It would send a sharp pain up through my leg that revived me for a spell so that I could continue with my preparations for supper.

The night that followed was one of uncomfortable and bitter memory. In my limited experience in the Rockefeller Mountains I had learned that if one has been working and has perspired at all he had best remove all his clothing before crawling into his sleeping bag. In my belamed and sore condition, any extra exertion was to be avoided so I wriggled down into the bag without changing from my travel clothes of the day. I had further noted that a good many polar sledgers had indicated that the most satisfactory way to dry one's socks was to put them inside one's shirt on his chest when he went to bed. It must be remembered that at low temperature even in the sun there is little evaporation of moisture such as perspiration, for the simple reason that the air will hold little or no moisture. Of course, when we stopped to make camp I had taken off my ski boots and my wet socks and had put my feet into the big canvas boots with the senna grass. Consequently my socks had long since become stiff from the moisture that had frozen in them. But I thought I had better follow the directions, as it were, so I pulled these cold clammy things into my bag and stuck them inside my shirt. I lay there and shivered an hour before I mustered enough energy to kick them down into the bottom of my bag and attempt to sleep. I usually found it sufficient after this to put my socks anywhere inside my sleeping bag when I turned in, to have them dried enough by morning so that I could put them on. Of course, this may have contributed to the necessity of turning my sleeping bag inside out more frequently than might otherwise have been necessary to dry it out, but this was much the lesser of the two evils.

Norman put a plaster on my heel the next morning and it was never again as bad as it had been on the second day, though it was more than two weeks before I could take a stride without being reminded of it.

The next or third day beyond depot number 2 was not so bad, and soon I found myself beginning to hope that I might after all master the technique of travelling on skis well enough to cover the thousand and more miles that lay ahead of us. And the dogs were a source of real inspiration too, for they were holding their own with greater energy than we had dared hope for. The young pups which were largely in the nature of an experiment were not only keeping up with the older dogs, but were ending the day with all kinds of reserve energy. The teams never stopped but that they were barking and tugging at their traces to be off again.

There was a heavy fall of hoar frost on the snow while we slept on the 12th. The sledges and skis dragged through it as though a layer of sand or cinders had been sprinkled on the surface, and there was a bitter wind dead ahead with the temperature 16 degrees below zero. It was a slow day and we had to watch for frozen faces and fingers continually. Even so we arrived at depot number 3 shortly after 3 o'clock.

The time had now arrived for us to give some thought to the precautions we should take to cross the crevasses not far ahead of us. We decided to combine Norman's and Mike's teams into one and have a long line connecting this double team with Freddy's team which would be in front. Mike, Freddy, Norman, and I would be roped together to manage this large unit and OB and Eddie would follow with their teams joined by a long line and they themselves would be roped together. This may read all right, and it sounded pretty feasible when we discussed it for we reasoned that by being joined in a long string, we could cross wider crevasse bridges in safety than otherwise. For if a roof broke, the chances were that only a part of a team or a man or two would fall in and the rest would pull him out. But no matter how well one knows his dogs, and no matter how well trained they may have been, they are still an uncertain quantity when they get into new and unfamiliar conditions.

Our progress was irritatingly slow. The dogs got tangled up much worse than ever and twice I added greatly to the congestion with my awkward attempts to help by falling down, and getting my skis all tangled up with the dog gear. Had the roof of a wide crevasse that we were crossing broken through, there is no telling how many of us would have been pulled to the bottom. We learned that safety lies in simplicity in the matter of roping ourselves together.

Though we could see the rough surface of the broken area for several miles ahead of us, we were really not in the crevassed zone until we reached latitude 81 degrees and 10 minutes south. First we came upon stagnant old cracks filled with ice and snow across which we drove with complete safety. As we travelled farther on, we found ourselves in a region where the crevasses were but partially roofed over or filled in; there were chasms here and there along our route. In places some of these older crevasses expanded into circular depressions from five to fifteen feet across, which looked a good deal like sink holes. We noted a few scattered haycocks in this part too, but these became thicker as we travelled farther into the zone of the disturbed ice. Some of the haycocks had steep sides and looked like great beehives and others were flatly conical in shape quite like those we had seen about the Bay of Whales, and they seemed to be identical with those we had studied there. Some of the beehive type at least, consisted of such a thin skin of ice that they could be broken through with a ski stick to reveal a great chasm below. It looked very much as though the circular sink-hole-like depressions may have formerly been the locations of these " beehives."

It was just beyond the typical haycock zone that the crevasses reached their maximum development. Though we sledged over or between them in safety we often held our breath. We passed over bridges with great ugly chasms stretching away on either side. We had crossed such a bridge with all of our teams once, and, just as the last sledge cleared the roof, down it fell to reveal a chasm some eight feet wide and so deep that the blueness of its depths seemed quite black. Of course, our crossing of this area was made much easier because the supporting party had pioneered the way and marked the trail.

With the uncertainty about getting across this broken area behind us, we could expect fairly safe going all the way to the mountains and as we clocked off the miles behind us our spirits rose. The two days immediately beyond the crevasses held a good deal of interest for us, for we were on the look-out for the evidence of land that Amundsen had reported toward the east of this locality. The supporting party had found no evidence of land either in going south or returning and we had the same experience. The 16th and 17th were bright and clear but we could see nothing to the east except the limitless desert of white which stretched along our eastern horizon in a flat, unbroken line. We were satisfied that there was no land nor appearances of land where Amundsen had reported it. From their observations made on the flight to lay a depot of fuel and food preparatory to the polar flight, Commander Byrd and his party corroborated our findings. Naturally, this discovery changed our plans formulated back in Little America to the extent that we did not have to plan to leave the trail when we were homeward bound to investigate this supposed land. This meant more time for us in the Queen Maud Mountains.

On the 17th we found the surface unaccountably soft. The dogs had to wallow along through the snow almost up to their bellies at times. It was so soft that the sledges sank into it and, of course, we found it hard to push our skis through it. There seemed to be a region here which is relatively free from strong winds else the snow would be packed. There is nothing in the geography hereabouts to suggest the slightest reason why this should be true, for in general the Antarctic is the windiest continent in the world.

Hard though the travelling was we sledged 14 miles to arrive at depot number 4.

The next few days were the most critical of our whole journey. So far the dogs had done great work but they had very evidently been hauling as heavy loads as we had any right to expect them to do. But shaving weights as closely as we could, we still had to attempt to leave this depot with an additional load of 80 pounds per team for this was the last outpost of the supporting party and they had left 500 pounds of dog food here for us. The morning of the 18th was filled with anxiety for us. Would the dogs do it?

Southward from here the shelf ice stretched away in unbroken solitude. From here on we had to break and mark the trail as we went along, which meant that more attention had to be given to the navigating. According to our pre-arranged plans Mike took his place out in front, and I drove alongside his front sledge looking to the dogs, watching the compass and calling out to him as seemed necessary, " Right," " Left," or " Steady." Mike had such a good sense of direction that at no time in our travels throughout the summer did he need much prompting from me. Eddie Goodale assumed the responsibility of putting down our trail-marking flags at half-mile intervals as we drove along, and he did a good job. I don't remember finding a single one of his flags blown down when we retraced our trail on the way home.

The events of that first day's drive beyond depot number 4 were so disheartening and dreary that I wanted to forget about them. The entry in my log for that day was of telegraphic brevity. I tried to beguile myself with the thought that it was an exceptional day and that the soft snow surface could not continue much farther. Mike had relieved his team by carrying fifty pounds of dog food on his back; Norman had carried his heavy pack and the rest of us had tugged away at ropes attached to the sledges in vain attempts to help the dogs along, yet our combined efforts for the whole day brought us only 9 miles nearer the mountains than we had been in the morning.

This was an interesting day for the great contrast that it showed between the old and the new methods of travel, when it came to the matter of getting some place in a hurry. About noon I heard Mike, who was ahead of me, yell, and looked up to see him pointing into the air. Immediately I could hear a familiar roar and looked up to behold the Floyd Bennett soaring over us southward bound to lay a depot of fuel and supplies for the polar flight party, and, as we thought at the time, dog food for us. As the plane passed over us a tiny parachute weighted with some messages that had come to us back in Little America, from the States, was dropped. We scarcely had time to say the proverbial " Jack Robinson " before the plane was out of sight; they were covering in about four hours a distance which it was to take us four weeks to cover.

On the next radio schedule I sent the following message back to Little America, thinking that the Commander had arrived there:

Commander Byrd:
It was a great sight to see you flying over us to-day but it made the mountains seem very far away stop our loads are far in excess of what the dogs can handle stop can we have ten

gallons gas at mountains and will you please tell me how much dog food you deposited for us? It will enable us to lighten our loads now which is so important stop several dogs will probably have to be killed within few days and our present plans call for cutting to eighteen dogs when we arrive stop we like our dogs very much and hope we won't have to kill so many cheerio and warm regards from all and best wishes for good luck on your polar flight.

Larry

It was not until three days later that we received the following message in reply and from which we, of course, derived but little comfort:

Ran out of gas on my way back and had to land eighty nautical miles from base stop fairly bad landing area but got away with it O.K. stop on account of gas leak had to use fifty gallons gas at mountains intended for base stop impossible to tell you how much gas we can leave at base because we might meet head winds stop however do best we can stop we leave here with greatly overloaded plane and are hard put to it for this reason stop however we will do all we possibly can for you but whole thing is so uncertain that you had better not depend on us at all stop left no dog food but did leave two hundred pounds man food which you can use if we come through O.K. Best to all you fellows from all of us stop please give us daily radio schedule for weather report.

Byrd

Though we had every reason to believe that the polar flight would come through safely, we dared not count on it absolutely. We were faced with the necessity of accomplishing what we had left Little America to do without any assistance from outside sources. This meant carrying out the plans we had made there in all their gruesome details.

I was awakened about four o'clock on the morning of the 19th by a curious squeaking noise that I could not account for. I crawled out of my fur bag and clambered out of the tent to investigate. I found that Belle had given birth to two puppies. This was a great surprise to me for I didn't know when we left Little America that she was contemplating motherhood, else we might have left her there. Now it was too late. I guess Belle herself realized the futility of trying to keep her pups for when I looked at her again a few minutes later they were gone and she was licking her chops. She had eaten them.

Even though 4 o'clock was an abnormally early hour for me to be up, I decided to stay up for I had planned to get up at 5 o'clock anyhow, in order to get some observations on the morning sun to get a check on our longitude. Twirling the screws of a theodolite is never pleasant work in the cold, and by the time I had finished my observations, my fingers were stiff and numb and I was well chilled generally. But it looked like such a good day to travel that I went to work getting breakfast for my five companions who were still asleep in their fur bags. It had been a cold night and I had to get my rock hammer to break the pots apart before I could start the cooker. Getting breakfast at 5 o'clock in the morning with the temperature at 15 degrees below zero, encased in clothes that have grown stiff in the cold while we slept, and with one's fingers seeming to be slowly freezing away is not exactly the kind of pastime one would seek for a picnic. It is all too easy to let one's mind dwell on the " luxury " of the life he has left behind, yet it is amazing how quickly one gets in the habit of taking these things as a matter of course and riding over such difficulties as though they did not exist. One is rarely if ever conscious of so-called hardships.

While breakfast was getting under way three more puppies were born to Belle, but it was so cold that they froze to death before we were ready to start. We were amazed to see this bitch, so lately a mother, tugging at her traces and barking to be off with the rest of the dogs.

We stopped about 9:30 to give the dogs a breathing spell and Belle took advantage of this halt to bring another babe into the world. This one had to be killed for there was no possible way to keep it, and again the mother was eager to be pulling with the other dogs. The almost passionate desire with which these huskies want to serve their masters is, I think, without parallel among beasts of burden. It was always a source of inspiration to me to watch them.

The surface was just as soft as it had been on the 18th. Everybody tried to help the dogs along with their heavy loads, even as we had on the preceding day. Our combined efforts netted us 15 miles and both the dogs and the men were worn and tired when we stopped.

The morning of the 20th was positively poisonous. I awoke to find the wind blowing 15 miles an hour from the southeast with the temperature 20 degrees below zero. Before I had gotten breakfast ready the wind had increased to 25 miles an hour and great wisps of snow were beginning their serpentine dance across the shelf ice. With no knowledge of the way ahead of us, we dared not travel under such conditions. Furthermore, it seemed to me to be a good chance to give everybody a day of rest, for we had been plodding along pretty steadily since we had left Little America on the 4th. I advised my companions about the weather and told them to spend the day in bed. The rest was good for both the men and the dogs, but when I got up at 6 o'clock on the morning of the 21st and found the wind still blowing I didn't like it. Time was precious and we had to get under way if it was at all possible. Fortunately the wind lulled before 9 o'clock and we were able to start.

The rest had literally given the dogs a new lease on life, and though the day was far from ideal for travelling, we covered 19 miles. A blanket of gray clouds made the visibility very poor as we started out, and presently the horizon disappeared completely and we found ourselves marching into a milky white wall. An opaque white gloom had settled over our world. The sastrugi were so numerous and so rough that we travelled as across a newly plowed field. This was one of the most tiring kinds of days to travel. It was hard to keep a proper sense of balance. I skied along watching the compass as usual and would occasionally level my eyes to see how Mike was keeping on the course but I wouldn't see him. Then I would suddenly discover that he was thirty or forty degrees up in the air, so it seemed at any rate, for one lost a sense of position.

The world was generally grotesque on such milky days but nothing seemed quite so completely out of proportion as one's sense of distance. There were no shadows at all, with the result that one could get no feeling for perspective. A tiny match box dropped on the snow a few feet away might look like a barn a mile distant. I once saw a huge rock exposure ahead of me on the homeward trail; it turned out to be old dog droppings. A depression near one's feet might be six inches or six feet deep and it might be six or sixteen feet away. However much these figures sound like exaggerations, anyone who has sledged in the Antarctic will know that I have understated the conditions.

Mike's lead dog, Tickle, was particularly obnoxious to-day. He was really too clever to be a lead dog anyhow. For the first two days after we had started our independent navigating with Mike travelling out in front, Tickle had very obediently followed right behind him. But he soon sensed my awkwardness on skis and came to know that no matter how much I might threaten him, I really could not reach him with my whip and could not catch up with him to beat him up without stopping the team.

" Gee, Tickle," I would yell, only to have him turn his head and grin at me, and then do quite as he pleased, and usually he pleased to go in exactly the opposite direction from that I had commanded. Occasionally he would get so careless that it was absolutely necessary to stop and take him to task with the whip. He knew precisely why it was being done and for quite a time afterwards was the best behaved dog in the whole pack. Then as the memory of the whip grew dim he began to get careless again.

However much we came to love our dogs there were yet times when they tried our patience beyond the limit of endurance. Norman had an uncanny ability of think-ing up new words to express his bad opinions of his dogs, without actually swearing at them. Never once did I hear him say " damn." As for the rest of us, I fear that word did occasionally escape our lips — in fact there were times when our comments to and about our dogs went far beyond the limits of that simple expletive.

It was with the greatest relief and satisfaction that we found ourselves at the location of our proposed depot number 5 in the middle of the afternoon of the 22nd, for with the caching of supplies to establish this depot our loads would be materially lightened. In fact we were able to work things out so well that we combined our dogs into four teams which in turn made it possible for us to abandon the two heavy rigid freight sledges which had been such a drag for Freddy's and OB's teams. This made a world of difference and we knew when we had gotten under way on the 23rd that the most gruelling part of our journey was behind us. We strode forward, for the first time since leaving Little America, with something besides hope to spur us on. Now we had confidence that we should arrive for we did not leave our new depot until noon but had covered 12 miles before 5 o'clock.

The polar flight party was getting impatient to complete their flight and were just waiting for the right weather, consequently we had frequent radio schedules to advise them of the weather where we were. I am sure Freddy was especially anxious to have the flight over, and of course the morning schedules slowed us up in getting under way but even so getting started in the morning was the slowest part of the whole day's work. We had long since settled ourselves to a fairly definite routine and there was little lost motion, but even without the radio schedule I would get up at 6 o'clock and still we never seemed to be able to start before 8:30. The morning radio schedule made us about an hour later.

The dogs seemed to be almost accumulating energy

these days. On the morning of the 24th they were unaccountably eager to go. There was no keeping them calm.
Perhaps they had caught the urge that was pushing us
on with the hope that we might arrive at the mountains
and the airplane base before the polar flight was made.
We knew that we should be of much greater assistance if
we could do this. At any rate in their eagerness to go
they seemed to outdo themselves this morning in getting
into the most inextricable tangles. The older dogs were
trained to wait for a word of command, but somehow the
pups had not learned about this, and sometimes two or
three of them would strain at their traces so hard that
they would start the whole load, which would slide up
onto the rest of the team and get the whole outfit into such
a muddle that it was sometimes necessary to unhitch the
whole team and start all over again.

The surface was particularly ragged today. Our course
lay transverse to hard sastrugi which here as everywhere
we had encountered them ran in a general southeast to
northwest direction. The wind had packed the snow so
hard that our skis and sledge runners made no noticeable
dents even on the sharpest ridges. We left no tracks
behind us that we could see. When the surface is so rough
the sledges bounce about a good deal and the compass
wobbles so much that it is extremely difficult to keep
an accurate check on the course.

The phenomenon of the shelf ice settling was particularly common and noticeable this day. We had long since
found that when we were sledging along over a new or
untrodden surface, now and then large areas of the snow
would suddenly give way beneath us. It felt as though
the ground was sinking from under us, and it gave one

a sort of sickening feeling until he got used to it. Such a sinking was usually followed by a muffled thud or roar, very rarely if ever by the sharp rifle-like crack that accompanies the parting of ice under strain. It startled us a good deal at first for we thought we were over buried crevasses and that the roofs were giving way beneath us. We soon learned not to be disturbed, for it became apparent that the whole thing was simply due to areas of the shelf ice settling a few inches under the strain of our weight upon it. But it was not so easy for the dogs to get accustomed to it, and it was often amusing to see them trying to shy away from a sound which they could not exactly locate.

So uncertain had I been about the straightness of our course on the 25th, due to the almost uselessness of the compass, that I got up at 5:30 on the morning of the 26th to get some sights on the sun for a line of position to check the course. My observations were reassuring. Bouncing about on the sastrugi had not seriously affected Mike's sense of direction for we had kept on the course very well, in spite of my inability to give very accurate guidance and direction with the compass.

This was a frightfully unpleasant morning, with the wind rising sometimes to as much as 20 miles an hour and picking up so much snow that we travelled along at times in a veritable snow fog. But it would have taken a thoroughgoing blizzard to stop us now, for we thought at noon that we could see the long-looked-for mountains. Sure enough, shortly afterward the southerly haze lifted, and there way off against the horizon to the southwest was a grand escarpment of snow-covered peaks but still nothing to be seen due south. But by four o'clock a huge mountain

loomed almost dead ahead of us. It was the most stimu-
lating afternoon we had known for many days for it was
a great relief to have something to steer towards at last.
And we had arrived at the location where we were to
build our depot number 6.

LUNCH IN THE SLOPES OF MT. NANSEN

Chapter VI

LAND!

" Mountains loom upon the path we take;
  Yonder peak now rises sharp and clear;
  Behold! it stands with its head uplifted,
  Thither we go since our way lies there."
                From the American Indian (Fletcher)

IT took us almost the whole forenoon of the 26th to
complete the stowing of supplies and the building of
the snow shelter around our depot number 6. Then, even
though there was a wind of from 20 to 30 miles per hour
on our port bow, we determined to go ahead.

It seemed as though the dogs had seen the mountains
too, and had come to share our eagerness to reach them,
for in spite of the stinging drift in their eyes they ran
along with their loads so easily that by 5 o'clock we had
covered 14 miles.

We thought it best to locate the polar flight supply base
as soon as we arrived at the mountains, or at least before
we established our own mountain depot. I had therefore
asked Commander Byrd to give me its location as accurately as possible. On our morning schedule I received
this message:

Gould:
  It is impossible for us to judge distances from those big
mountains by eye but our base appears to be about ten to

fifteen miles west of Axel Heiberg stop distances as estimated may be very much in error stop if you get to the mountains before we fly it will be big help as the landing field we picked out is quite rough with hard sastrugi stop we were flying over towards Carmen Land to get good glimpse of Axel Heiberg Glacier and perhaps of Carmen Land when we found gas running low from abnormal consumption and had to turn back stop this is very unfortunate stop our very best to you and the boys will drop a letter from the plane.

Byrd

On the morning of the 27th the wind still continued with heavy drift, but the polar flight party was so eager to take off that Commander Byrd requested us to give them a radio schedule at 1 o'clock, in the hope that by that time we would be able to report good weather. Our weather had improved very greatly by that time, but we learned that conditions had grown more unfavorable at Little America. There the sky was heavily overcast and there was a good deal of drift. It was not possible for the plane to take off so we broke camp and were shortly on our way.

It looked as though our bad weather was moving northward for as conditions improved with us they had grown less favorable at Little America. Our weather became increasingly calm and clear as the day lengthened. There was never more than a slight breeze throughout the afternoon so we were able to see the mountains, toward which we were steering, the whole time. In mid afternoon we saw a great gap in the high mountain wall which we thought must be Axel Heiberg Glacier. It was to the right of our course but we altered our course nevertheless, so as to head directly toward it.

The day ended with perfect weather and there was never a more beautiful morning than that of the 28th which followed. I informed Bill Haines about the perfection of our weather and the fact that the barometer was steady so that we might expect it to continue so. I also sent the following message to Commander Byrd:

Glad to stand by and help with polar flight this looks like the day stop can you send me on twelve o'clock schedule longitude and latitude of mountain base the mountains look much nearer to us than they should stop the good wishes of all of us go with you.

Larry

We were requested to remain in camp and wait for a noonday radio schedule with Little America, and at that time there came the following message:

Gould:
We expect to shove off about three or four o'clock stop guess you had better stand by until flight is over stop sorry to ask this stop if there is any change in weather between now and our time of leaving let us know stop better keep frequent schedules between now and then.

Byrd

The Commander also had the Little America operator tell us that further information about the mountain base they had established would be dropped to us when the plane flew over us. Some days before he also indicated that a number of aerial photographs of the mountains taken by Captain McKinley on the base laying flight would be dropped too. I was eager to see these photographs for I expected them to be of considerable assistance in formulating plans for our geological work.

Since one of the functions of the geological party was that of a potential relief expedition to the polar flight party, we had worked out plans for operation in case our services were needed in this capacity. Naturally these plans were based upon the assumption that radio communication between the parties concerned would be interrupted. Assuming good communication by radio all plans for rescue would naturally be arranged between the two parties by mutual assent. Otherwise our emergency plans were to be as follows:

" Since the radio note of the polar plane will be audible to the geological party as well as to the base at Little America, it is safe to assume that the abrupt termination of the sound or note of the plane, means an accident to the plane. Because of the fact that the course over which the plane is presumably flying will be known to all parties before the flight, a rough check can be gotten as to the place where the forced landing occurred. Both the geological party and all hands at Little America and any other parties that may be in the field, will stand by until enough time has elapsed without the plane having been sighted by any party to demonstrate that a forced landing has occurred. Before any action is taken the geological party will get in communication with the base at Little America, provided this is possible within a reasonable length of time. This is desirable both in order to inform the base of its plans for rescue and to give any desired instructions for coöperation from that quarter.

1. If the forced landing occurs between Little America and the base at the mountains, the rescue will be made from Little America, unless the forced landing is much nearer the mountains.

2. If the forced landing occurs between the mountain base and the South Pole, places of rendezvous to which the geological party will first proceed are necessary.

Assuming that Amundsen's notions about the geography are fairly correct, there seem to be two places that can be found without great difficulty by either party. These are Mt. Betty at the foot of Axel Heiberg Glacier and Mt. Helland Hanssen which occupies a fairly isolated situation on the plateau, beyond the Queen Maud Range proper.

A sufficient time having elapsed and the geological party having communicated its plans to the base it will proceed directly to Mt. Betty. There they will leave a cache of food and in some conspicuous place in the cache will deposit detailed instructions as to where they have gone and what their plans are. The cache will if possible be built on the south side of the mountain and marked with flags, rocks and anything that will make it especially conspicuous from that side.

" After leaving Mt. Betty the geological party will proceed up Axel Heiberg Glacier, following Amundsen's route to the top, where it will diverge to the west and go as directly as possible to the south end of Mt. Helland Hanssen. Here again a well marked cache of food with details about plans, etc., will be left on the south side of the mountain.

" Naturally the landed party will proceed directly to this part of Mt. Helland Hanssen, if the landing occurred between it and the South Pole or very near to it in any other direction. If the forced landing occurs farther north, it will proceed toward Mt. Betty. If they arrive at either place ahead of the geological party they will either wait or build a well marked cairn and leave in it details regarding their plans. Should they arrive and find the cairn and cache built by the rescue party they will have a general notion at least of when and how they can expect assistance.

" When a searching party believes itself to be within three days march of any possible positions of the lost party, it will in case of reasonably good visibility light a smoke bomb at 12 o'clock noon, 180th meridian time. Both parties will be on the lookout for signals at this time especially, and should the smoke signal of the rescue party be recognized by those lost, they should answer immediately by setting off a smoke bomb. If it developes that enough smoke bombs can be carried, this same procedure will be repeated at 6 P.M., 180th meridian time. If the rescue party is fairly certain that it is within striking distance of the lost party, it should not proceed in very thick weather for fear of missing it.

" Parties in the field as well as the plane party should be equipped with a small kite made of orange colored cloth. Attempts should be made to fly this both at noon and at 6 P.M. and naturally whenever it is possible to do so, kites should be kept in the air."

Though we were 15 miles from the place where we had planned to build our depot number 7, we decided to make use of the wait necessitated by the polar flight by building it here. The accompanying side flags were set and the snow beacon with its cache of precious supplies was built while we waited, and thus our stop was not a complete subtraction from our travelling time.

At 3:39 Freddy shouted to us that the plane had taken off at Little America and that he could hear its radio note very plainly. Toward the end of the afternoon we began to look rather anxiously toward the north for it and about 8 o'clock we heard the roar of the motors and shortly saw the plane well to the west of us. They appeared to see us almost simultaneously and altered their course so as to pass nearer to us. At 8:15 they zoomed low over us by way of salute and within a few brief minutes were out of sight on their way. As they passed over us a little door opened in the bottom of the plane and out dropped a message parachute which we ran to pick up.

As we had studied the mountains ahead of us toward the end of our travel on the 27th we had come round to the belief, and even conviction, that the great glacier toward which we had altered our course was after all not Axel Heiberg but Liv. When the plane disappeared from our view we thought it had gone toward Axel Heiberg; we got this impression on account of the position it had to assume to make good its course and at the same time buck a strong easterly wind. It had, however, gone toward Liv to make its climb up onto the plateau.

We had a good time examining the contents of our message parachute for it was rather novel and almost exciting — this business of getting air mail so many thousands of miles farther south than it had ever been delivered before. For in addition to some cigarettes, some additional films and an extraordinarily interesting array of aerial photographs from Captain McKinley, there were some radiograms from friends back in the states forwarded to us from Little America, and lastly letters from our friends there, duly stamped and addressed as for instance this one from Dr. Coman:

> Larry Gould
> Geological Party
> En Route Queen Maud Range
> BYRD ANTARCTIC EXPEDITION

There was another one addressed to

> Dr. Laurence M. Gould
> Camp Michigan-Harvard-Yale-Wisconsin
> Antarctica

Harrison, the ever thoughtful chap, remembering that we might be interested in the world of sport, had sent me a small envelope with a bit of paper containing all of the football scores that had been received at Little America. Ordinarily these would have interested me only more or less casually, but it happened that we knew that Harvard and Michigan were to play on November 14th, and Goodale, Vaughan and Crockett, all from Harvard, had been telling me all the way from Little America how Harvard played football, and what they were going to do to my own alma mater on that occasion. Naturally under such circumstances I could never have forgiven Michigan had they not acquitted themselves with credit. Never did anyone anywhere view the results of a football game with more satisfaction and even relief than did I read the results of that one — some 400 miles from the South Pole out in the midst of the bleakest desert in all the world — Michigan 14, Harvard 12! The subject of football was not brought up again throughout the whole summer — that is by Norman or Eddie or Freddy.

None of us was able to relieve Freddy at the radio, for he alone understood its operation sufficiently well to know what was going on. But even he was beset with a new and unexpected difficulty in this case, for all the messages from the polar plane back to Little America were sent by code. This code had been devised after our departure from Little America, and of course we did not know what it was all about, and no copy of it was dropped to us from the plane. Freddy copied down such queer sounding jargon as this:

" encore, janitor, frenchman, onalaska, etc."

As the plane got farther and farther south, the word " sugar " recurred with increasing frequency, from which Freddy assumed that it must mean " South Pole." We later learned that he was right.

When I crawled out of my bag on the morning of the 29th I found Freddy with heavy eyes, but still with the ear phones on his head. He told me that the plane had refuelled at the mountain base and was on its way back to Little America. But we had expected no mishap, for the Floyd Bennett was being manned by a great crew.

I started the cooker and when the snow had melted enough to make our tea, I called all hands and we went about the morning work of the camp, getting ready to start as soon as the polar flight was finished. At 9:10 Freddy told us that the plane had landed at Little America. We tried to be the first to send our congratulations but in the excitement nobody was listening for us at Little America and we were unable to raise them. We were just a little piqued that all of the radio communication from the plane had been in code that we could not understand so we had devised a code to send our congratulations. In the following message which we sent " blind " and which, unfortunately, was never received, are the gratulatory good wishes of the geological party to our colleagues of the polar flight party:

For Polar Party WFA:
  Dog chain gee pole gangline janitor onalaska wooden runners thrall Liv Glacier fatimas velvet cheerio skoal
Geological Party

The day of enforced idleness for the polar flight gave both the men and the dogs a most welcome rest, except Freddy Crockett, who was necessarily exempt from the rest period because of his radio duty.

Being not completely played out, as had so frequently been the case for so many days in the past, the dogs were restless on the night of the polar flight. Finally as a proclamation of his uneasiness, Scott pointed his muzzle straight into the sky and started to howl as only a husky knows how to howl. Not to be outdone, Dinny, Fitz Green, then Al Smith and Wilkins, added their voices to Scott's, and gradually all of the dogs took up the cry. There may be no reason why this canine chorus should be so strangely in keeping with the bleakness of this lifeless world of ice, yet it always seemed to be so to me. Hearing them again, after nights of silence when they had been too tired even to howl, I found I had greatly missed this evening choir. Their howls were never unmusical to my ear and our dogs had been on the road together so long, had " sung " so much in unison, that they now howled in the same key! Then suddenly, with all the precision of a symphony orchestra leader bringing an overture to a close, the howling stopped, and stopped cleanly; not one voice trailed after. Who signalled them to stop, how they did it, or why, I could never understand.

We had become very fond of our dogs and had come to know each other very well. I do not believe there is any kind of dog in the world more friendly than these huskies generally are. I never saw dogs more responsive to kindness and attention. They invited it, and no matter how hard we had driven them, how mercilessly we had forced them on, they were never too tired to respond to a friendly gesture from their masters.

Time was precious and we were all refreshed and eager to go, with the exception of Freddy, but he insisted that he could do his day's trek without sleep. And he did do it! We struck our tents, lashed our sledges and were ready to start by 10 o'clock. Mike Thorne, on his skis, pushed out in the lead as always. Since we had but four teams now I did not have to drive, so I skied alongside O'Brien's front sledge which was in the lead and upon which we had mounted the boat compass. Next came Norman Vaughan with his team, then Edward Goodale and lastly Freddy. It was great to see the dogs so extraordinarily full of energy; they were tugging at their traces, eager to be under way. We needed to say " Yake," which in our dog vernacular meant " Get up," but once and they were off, and of course almost at once began the eternal task of disentangling them. Dogs simply will not stay put. They are forever playing leap-frog over one another and getting their traces tangled with those of their team mates and with the gangline to which they are all hitched. They sometimes get into the most complicated messes and it is no soft job straightening them out, especially on cold mornings.

It seemed so warm when we started out this morning that Mike did not put his windproof parka over his heavy woolen shirt. He had become a curious sight when I came up alongside him in the middle of the forenoon. The temperature of the air was low enough so that the perspiration from his body was not dissipated into the air, but collected as rime or hoar frost in and upon his shirt. Hair-like strings of the frost clung to his shirt in such masses that he looked like a polar bear.

The mountains stood out so distinctly as we started out that we could not believe that they were still 50 to 60 miles away. It looked to be a comparatively easy two days' trek. And what a glorious sight they were — what a reward for the 400 miles of sledging across the almost unchanging flatness of the great Ross Shelf Ice. In front of us and vanishing to the right and to the left into the horizon, there rose against a cold blue sky a mighty clear-cut façade of massive tabular ice clad mountains. Looming up sheerly from the shelf ice, which was here but 250 feet above sea level to heights of 8, 10, and even 15 thousand feet, with their blankets of never trodden snow and ice, they were creations of unsurpassed majesty and beauty; wild and rugged in their splendor, but always beautiful. And soaring above all the rest was one great snow-bright top which we guessed and wanted to find to be Mt. Fridtjof Nansen. Later we found that we had guessed rightly.

As the day passed, the mountains drew so much nearer that when we thought we had covered half the distance to them from our stop of the preceding night, we halted and made camp.

We were able to establish communication with Little America and send our belated congratulations to the polar flight group, and of course we were all pleased to have the following radiogram:

Larry:

Your dope on weather is what made our flight possible stop I just want you to know what a supreme contribution you have made to the success of our flight stop we left at base ten gallons of gas about 200 pounds of food twenty gallons oil blow torch and lot of empty cans stop there is a flag on top of food pile stop awfully sorry that we couldn't leave more stop we had a terrible struggle with our heavy load stop will radio you later about extraordinary mountain formations we saw.

Byrd

The sun was brilliant and the sky was cloudless when I pulled myself out of my fur bag at 5 o'clock on the morning of the 30th. It was just the sort of day we wanted and needed for we anticipated crevasses across our path before the day ended. This was one anticipation that we realized to its fullest extent.

In due time the oatmeal and tea were ready, and after some coaxing and more threatening on my part, everyone was up. Soon they had gathered inside the cook tent and were huddled around the cooker for their ration of oatmeal, tea, and biscuits. Time was too precious to indulge in the luxury of lingering over our food; it was soon bolted and the cook tent emptied. While the rest were packing the other two tents and harnessing and hitching their dogs, I fixed a vacuum jug of hot tea for the noon day stop and then put away the cooking gear and cooker. By 8 o'clock we were all packed and ready for our last day's travel to the foot of the mountains. They looked so near that we all knew it would be an easy day. None of us thought the distance to be more than 15 miles. In sheer fun I said to my companions: " We'll make the mountains to-day or bust." It came all too near being the latter.

We were soon to learn that our estimates of distances in the Antarctic were apt to be more misleading than helpful. There are two very evident reasons why this is true. The most obvious one is the absence of trees or any kind of familiar object whatever, by which one habitually estimates such things in more temperate home latitudes. Secondly is the extraordinary clearness of the Antarctic air when the sun is high and all the clouds and mists have been dispelled. Davies brought with him a device for counting the dust particles in the air. He made such counts while crossing the Pacific en route to New Zealand

and of course carried on the work in the Antarctic. He found that the air over the middle of the Pacific Ocean was about twice as dusty as was that over the Antarctic Continent — and nobody thinks of the Pacific Ocean as being an especially dusty place!

The dogs were somewhat less eager to start on this morning of the 30th of November, but they were no less eager to get themselves into the most inextricable tangles. It seemed hours before we had them all organized and were settled down to the steady grind of the day's work. But the surface was good and everything went along all right, except that the mountains began to retreat. At any rate the distance between them and us did not seem to lessen as we approached. Shortly before noon what had been a mild breeze from the south became a very real wind that lashed at our faces and held us back perceptibly. By the time we stopped for lunch it had developed into a veritable Antarctic blizzard. Lunch was sort of a bitter trial; we could find no shelter in which to drink our two cups of tea and bolt our chocolate and biscuits. Some crouched behind the sledges, and others walked up and down to keep warm as they ate and drank. But in spite of our discomfort, we were all amazed to find this wind relatively warm — I mean as compared with other winds that we had been subjected to from this direction. Throughout our journey southerly winds had been the bitterest that we had encountered. It would have been folly if not impossible to have driven against such a wind as we were facing this day, when we were 100 miles farther north on the shelf ice. It was far and away the warmest southerly wind we had ever faced and grew warmer as we neared the mountains. Our discomfort was not due primarily to its low temperature but to its high velocity.

The dogs were very reluctant to start after lunch, and some had to be persuaded with the whip. We did not like this but we had to go on. Little pellets of hard snow in the teeth of the heavy wind felt like gravel being hurled into our faces, and the wind was ever on the increase. Shortly after noon it had increased so greatly in velocity that even Mike could no longer ski against it. He had to fall back and be helped along beside a sledge like the rest of us. The dogs grew weary and had to be prompted with the whip from time to time.

About 2 o'clock I turned around to see if all the teams were coming along behind us, and was startled to see but two. With some qualms I called a halt to discover what was wrong, and suddenly, the other team appeared as from nowhere. Then only did I realize that the shelf ice was no longer level but had been pushed up into great rolls, so gentle and so far apart that we did not know we were crossing them — yet they were high enough to hide a dog team between them.

Now and then we crossed a narrow crevasse. Soon they multiplied and ran transverse to our course. But the danger from them was lessened by the fact that by 3 o'clock the air had become quite clear. The wind had not abated in the least but the surface had become half icy and there was no loose snow for it to pick up. The sledges were much harder to handle on the slippery surface, but we could see our way and that is all important when one is travelling among crevasses.

The drivers were pushing their dogs for all they could stand now. O'Brien, with whom I was driving in the lead, had to urge his team ahead constantly, and when the other drivers came close to us I could hear them shouting to their dogs. Norman talked ceaselessly to his team, now he pleaded, now he threatened. " Yake, Dinny," " Get up, Dingo," I could hear him say. And from Freddy: " Quimbo, you son-of-a-gun, get in there and pull! " Eddie was always fairly quiet in his exhortations.

As we proceeded we found the crevasses closer together, wider and more persistent; they did not seem to play out either to the right or left of us. They were getting much more formidable than we had ever anticipated. Once in a while we crossed over one which a few feet away was open to disclose a yawning chasm. We began to go more slowly and O'Brien and I picked our way with increasing care.

It did not relieve our feelings the least bit to realize too late that we might have partially avoided these crevasses by altering our course more to the east. We had decided to start our mountain survey at Liv Glacier and hence had kept on this course. One of the aerial photographs that Captain McKinley had dropped to us on the polar flight showed the actual area we were crossing. We noticed that the ice was crossed by an extensive series of straight evenly spaced parallel lines. Their distribution was so regular that I was sure that they were due to scratches in the film; I had never heard of, much less seen a system of crevasses of such perfectly uniform and widespread development. Now we were learning too late that the supposed scratches were really mammoth crevasses.

The afternoon wore on with the dogs becoming more tired and the crevasses more ominous. I looked back at frequent intervals to satisfy myself that the other teams

were following closely. Norman's team seemed to be dragging behind, and presently he had dropped back so far
that we stopped and waited for him to come up to us.
When he arrived, there were but eight dogs in harness.
Lady, one of the best and most faithful, had worn out
and was now being carried on the sledge. It had never
been necessary to use the whip on Lady, and now she
had literally pulled her life out for us. She had fallen
in harness, bleeding at the mouth. When I went up to
the sledge to give her a friendly pat, she could scarcely
raise her head, and whined in a piteous fashion. I think
she realized that she had pulled her last time for us, and
yet I hope she did not know, for she would have to be
killed at the end of the day. We did not want to take
time then to end her misery, and besides, her carcass had
to be carried on; it would make food for the other dogs.
Heartless as that may seem, it would have been the sheerest folly, out here 400 miles from Little America, to have
wasted anything that might ever be useful as food for
either man or dog.

On we went, talking, shouting, and goading the dogs;
we could not stop. There was no place. The morning's
jest, that we would make the mountains or bust, had become an almost grim necessity. Nowhere could we anchor
a tent peg nor stake out the dogs on the glare ice, and
on every side were crevasses. Our best judgment prompted
us to clear them before we made camp and so on we went.

Some of the crevasses were from 50 to 100 feet wide,
but so far we had found them roofed over, in places at
least, so that we had dared to cross. Safety precautions
were difficult to devise for this kind of travelling. With
the surface so slippery it was out of the question for us

to rope ourselves together and still attempt to manage the dogs and sledges. We later decided that the safest procedure in such extensive crevasses as these was to tie long ropes onto the rear of the sledges. We hung onto the free ends of these ropes and drove the teams ahead of us. If they cleared the roof of a crevasse with their loaded sledges it seemed a pretty safe bet that it was strong enough to support us. Hanging onto the rope, we slid across on skis, swinging out to one side so as not to cross the roof in the exact spot where it had been weakened by the dogs and sledges. We reasoned that if a roof collapsed with us upon it, the team on the farther side would support us until we could be hauled out. It was most astonishing to see how the dogs would flatten themselves to the ground and dig in with their toes to hold themselves from slipping.

More than once in the course of the afternoon our lead team would cross a crevasse in safety with us, only to have the roof fall in behind us. We then stopped and waited for the rest to guide them to a safer route.

Good old Pete, O'Brien's lead dog, soon learned that it was safest to cross a crevasse in the shortest way possible. Our course lay transverse to the general direction of the largest crevasses and Pete, on coming to one, invariably changed his course so as to cross at right angles. But having crossed in safety himself, he seemed to have little thought for the rest of the team and the sledges they were hauling behind them. Immediately he was well up on solid ice on the further side, he would shift back to the proper course and thus drag the rest of the dogs and the sledges transversely across.

We had passed over so many crevasses, had seen so

many bridges collapse about us that we felt we must surely be done with the worst of them. It was this hope that ever lured us on, for 6 o'clock found us in a maze of chasms and cracks that made those we had already crossed seem puny. We stopped and had a cold bite to eat. The dogs dropped in their tracks and were almost immediately asleep. Had we thought it even half way safe we would have made camp for the day right there. But we were not sure that we were not over a great crevasse and we knew that if such were the case the roof was growing weaker every time we moved. The ice underfoot seemed solid. But that is just the trouble when one is in the midst of such a maze of crevasses. One never knows where a piece may fall in and disclose a bottomless pit. It was not safe to linger there.

The sledge meter registered 29 miles and the rocks seemed so near — looked as though one might almost reach out and touch them. To go back over the way we had come far enough to reach solid ice was a long way; the dogs would never have stood it, nor did we have the heart to attack it ourselves. I don't think anyone of us would have given a great deal for his chances of retracing our steps in safety. It was inconceivable that conditions could be worse ahead. Was there not a general in the Boer War who, in the midst of an uncertain but fairly hopeless battle, said, " If we go back it means defeat; if we go forward we die. We shall go forward." Our position was probably not critical in that sense but then for months we had planned this; we had set our faces to reach the Queen Maud Mountains. We would not, we could not turn back, even temporarily. We had to go forward and everything had to give way to that necessity.

Could we have helped the dogs a bit with the sledges it would not have been quite so hard, but the surface was so icy that we had to cling to the sledges just to keep upright on our skis. To aid in pulling was out of the question. It was, undeniably, cruelty to drive the dogs any farther, but we had to go on. No other course was open to us with an equal degree of safety. It was hard to get the dogs onto their feet again. I turned my head to avoid seeing the drivers wielding their heavy whips; but it had to be done. Finally they were up and slowly got under way, to pull for us as long as they could strain a muscle. One of the depressing things about such hard sledging with the dogs is that one must stifle his finer feelings to the necessity immediately before him.

It was interesting to see the dogs, and especially the pups, attempting to quench their thirst as we sledged along over the ice. Ordinarily they grabbed a bite of snow from time to time as they ran along, and without slackening their pace at all. They couldn't do that with the ice, and the pups who had never known anything but snow, were especially disgruntled at the necessity that made them lick the ice whenever we stopped. They had tried to bite it at first, just as they had the snow, but they soon found that licking it was the easier way.

Our route continued across great partially covered crevasses that stretched away to the right and to the left as far as we could see. We had to continue to cross them for there was no going around. Many were at least 100 feet wide and had apparently been roofed over for a long time. These wide roofs had sagged in the middle thus pulling away from the sides, leaving open or thinly roofed spaces from a few inches to three or four feet in width, that seemed to be without bottom. We were able to slide over these because of our long skis, but it was not so easy for the dogs. Individuals were always partially breaking through the thin roofs or falling in bodily to hang suspended in their harnesses until the forward surge of the team dragged them out.

As we went on, the surface became more icy and slippery; it was increasingly difficult to manage ourselves on skis — and the crevasses were as large and as close together as ever. Just as O'Brien and I cleared an especially big one the whole surface fell away behind us. Where we had crossed but a second earlier was now a yawning chasm, large enough to have swallowed our entire party.

This seemed to be sort of an angry parting shot, for though the surface shortly became so slick that we could not stand on our skis but had to take them off and ride on the sledges, the crevasses became less formidable. The terrain sloped slightly toward the mountains, hence our additional weight did not add a great deal to the dogs' burdens, and the mountains now really were within reach.

For the first time in many hours we began to breathe more easily. We began to look about us for a patch of snow on which we could stake our dogs and anchor our tents. At 9:30 we found it and stopped to make camp. The dogs fell in their tracks and were practically asleep before they hit the snow. We were scarcely less tired. The sledge meter showed that we had travelled not 15 but exactly *40 miles*. And half of that had been across a frozen inferno the like of which we had not encountered in all the trek across the Ross Shelf Ice and never did find again in all of our summer in the mountains.

We decided to have a hot supper before we went to

bed and of course the cooker seemed to work with tantalizing slowness; it seemed an age before we were squatted about it inside the cook tent ready for our hoosh. One of the boys with his spoon half way to his mouth suddenly dropped off to sleep. His bowl of pemmican slipped from his fingers and spattered over the man beside him. We were all just about as tired but we had arrived. It was a moment for which we had been living. We were camped in the very shadow of our long sought mountains and *we had reached land!* I was the only one of the six of us who had seen, much less set foot upon any land since we had passed Scott Island way out in the Ross Sea en route to the Antarctic during the preceding year. At Little America we had lived and worked on the top of a great floating sheet of ice and except for a few miles at most, our journey to the Queen Maud Mountains had in the same sense been over the water.

On the morrow my companions would set foot upon the rocks for the first time since they left Dunedin New Zealand, exactly one year before.

CHAPTER VII

MT. FRIDTJOF NANSEN

I live not in myself, but I become
Portion of that around me; and to me
High mountains are a feeling, but the hum
Of human cities torture;

BYRON

THE mountains were formed on such a gigantic scale
that, in spite of our vicissitudes in reaching them on
the last day of our march, we had begun to form definite
notions about their structure and general make-up from
as much as 20 miles away. We could distinguish an array
of ragged, angular peaks and ridges in the foreground, and
behind them and towering far above them great flat
topped tabular mountains. Though extensive exposures of
bare rocks were rare, they were yet numerous enough
to enable me to deduce that the huge tabular mountains,
like Mt. Fridtjof Nansen, were covered with great thicknesses of flat or nearly flat-lying rocks, which were quite
different in appearance from the rocks of the ragged peaks
of the fore hills. When we were still many miles away
from Liv Glacier and the foot of the range, I had become
convinced that these great tabular mountains held the
key to the geological story of it all. They looked to me
like a vast series of sedimentary rocks, that is the kind
deposited in layers or strata, and these layers are the pages

of the book of geology, for from them we largely interpret the history of the earth. We decided that our very first task would be to ascend the range somewhere so that we could reach these flat-lying rocks.

Another early impression of the mountains that we retained was that there were almost more glaciers than mountains; for not only is the continuity of the range broken up by the great valley or outlet glaciers such as Liv and Axel Heiberg, but every little pocket or niche in the mountain front had its own individual mountain glacier. Some of these attained considerable size.

In spite of the lesson we had received on the previous day about our inability to estimate distance accurately in the brilliantly clear air of the Antarctic, I was still not prepared to find that the rocks under which we had pitched our tents, and which I expected to examine casually after breakfast, were still more than a mile away — yet they were. Still undaunted I thought we should be able to climb up Liv Glacier to a rocky mass that divided it near its head and which was capped by the coveted flat-lying rocks. Accordingly, on the morning of December 1st, Mike, O'Brien, and I strapped crampons onto our heavy ski boots, roped ourselves together, and prepared to ascend the glacier.

We climbed alongside a rock wall on the way and found that it was composed of the very oldest rocks known in the world. They were dark colored granites and gneises and associated rocks which are known to the geologist as the pre-Cambrian. It was at once evident to us, as we looked about, that the ragged peaks of the foot hills were formed from these ancient rocks. In many places their solid dark color was broken up by light colored quartz veins which we examined in vain for minerals of any consequence.

We were all amazed to find tiny pools of water near the first rocks we came to, for the air temperature had not risen to the thawing point. There was abundant evidence that a considerable greater amount of melting took place later in the summer when the sun was higher and the rocks had absorbed more heat from it.

We climbed the first mile or two up the glacier without too much difficulty and then we began to get into a good deal of soft snow. This was not pleasant for in places it was but a blind for buried crevasses and without sensing its presence at all, I stepped right onto the thin roof of such a crevasse. As it gave way I fell forward and caught the far wall with my arms and pulled myself out. The Lord only knows how deep these great gashes in the ice were. I turned and looked down the bare ice walls to the blue-black depths beyond which my vision failed and agreed with Mike that it would be safer to wear skis when climbing about such places.

There is no exaggerating the extraordinary value of skis both as a means of getting over the snow in a hurry and as a great additional factor of safety. The crevasses into which I had fallen could doubtless have been crossed on skis without mishap. We had not brought them with us this morning for the route up the glacier from our camp seemed to be one of nothing but glare ice. We soon learned that it was only along steep slopes that the bluish slick ice of the glaciers showed through the overlying mantle of snow. Even as skis had been the most important factor in enabling us to reach the mountains, it appeared that they would continue to be the safest and most efficient means of getting us over the glaciers and among the peaks.

The rock mass toward which we had started to climb seemed to remain always about the same distance up the glacier ahead of us. The snow was entirely too deep and soft for us to continue our climb without skis so we decided to cross the glacier and try the other side. Shortly our way was barred by thinly roofed crevasses of unthinkable size. A house could have been dropped into any one of them without leaving any trace whatever.

Discouraged and further disillusioned as to our inability to estimate distances, we had to turn back toward our camp. By rough triangulation the next day we learned that the rocky top we had hoped to reach easily in one day's climb was 21 miles up the glacier and would have necessitated a climb upward of at least a mile over crevasses and ice falls that could scarcely be more formidable. After this experience we decided that Mike's notion for estimating distance was about the most reliable. It was to look ahead, guess the distance, multiply that figure by two and then add ten!

One thing that had interested us greatly in our short and almost futile climb was that the lower part of the glacier was pushed back into great rolls or waves of ice. We discovered as we looked out over the shelf ice that these rolls or waves were really continuations of the ones we had crossed to reach the mountains. Furthermore, they were not crescentic to the front of the glacier, that is they were not caused by it, but rather seemed to have been formed by some gigantic force or flow from an easterly direction. A force with so powerful a push that it had triumphed over the ice stream of Liv Glacier, great as it was, and had pushed it back into rolls or waves. Imagine the huge waves that are backed up into a river mouth against its forward flow by the heavy swells set up by a passing ship, and one has a picture of how the lower part of Liv Glacier looked. These rolls or waves were unbelievably large; some were as much as 500 feet high from trough to crest.

In its upper reaches Liv Glacier looked not unlike a river consisting of falls and rapids with short stretches of calmer waters, all suddenly become rigid. Ice flows and behaves a good deal like water, and if one can imagine such a paradox as a turbulent stream flowing at the rate of but a few feet a year, he has a suggestive notion of what such a glacier as Liv is like.

The results of this first day in the mountains were so discouraging that I sent a radiogram back to Commander Byrd at Little America that night, to the effect that it might take us all summer just to achieve our first goal — that of ascending the range high enough to find the meaning of the big flat-topped mountains. Over our evening hoosh we discussed ways and means and finally decided that we could not possibly find a worse place to penetrate the mountains by going further eastward. We were even sure that there was at least one better way, and that was Axel Heiberg Glacier up which Amundsen had climbed on his way to the pole, and Amundsen nor anyone else could have ascended Liv Glacier. The polar flight party had flown up Liv Glacier on the way to the South Pole and down Axel Heiberg on their return, and I, therefore, asked Commander Byrd for any information he might be able to give us by radio as to the relative accessibility of these two routes for dog teams. On the 3rd I received this message from him:

Larry:

Think you are right about Axel Heiberg Glacier Liv appears to me to be impossible because of crevasses stop you can make it up Amundsen's way and can reach Mt. Nansen.

Byrd

This message was reassuring for Mt. Fridtjof Nansen was the one mountain that we most wanted to reach. It was the most distinctive feature in the whole mountain system so far as we could see. Its broad flat top was capped with a great thickness of the desired rocks and finally the patches of exposed rock seemed more extensive on the slopes of this mountain than on any other, and from afar it appeared that it would be at least as easy to climb as any of the rest.

We spent one more day at our Liv Glacier camp so that Thorne and O'Brien could start their surveying work and so I could have another day for collecting rocks in this vicinity; for even though we had marked our trail through the crevasses, upon the assumption that we would retrace our steps when we started back toward Little America, we were about decided that such a course would be too hazardous; we should never pass this way again but would strike out from the mountains when the time to depart came, by some new, and we hoped, less dangerous route. We also wanted to locate the cache of food left by the polar flight party before we established our own mountain base or depot number 8.

Since it had been windy almost continuously in this

our first mountain camp, we thought it must be just a local condition due to our nearness to Liv Glacier, and that when we really got under way toward the east we might find better weather. But it was not so. We broke camp on the morning of the 3rd and headed out from the mountains to make a search for the airplane cache. We headed into a gusty sort of wind blowing from 15 to 35 miles an hour, with the result that we were travelling now into a writhing wall of blinding drift and again, when the wind lulled, into relatively fair weather. We anticipated little difficulty in locating the desired cache, for among the aerial photographs dropped to us from the plane on the polar flight, was one with its location plainly marked on it. We carefully followed the bearings indicated on this photograph but still we didn't find the depot, and thinking that possibly the members of the base laying party, like us, had greatly underestimated the distance from the mountains, we thought it might be much farther out on the shelf ice than the photograph showed it to be. We therefore sledged 10 miles outward in a vain search and finally made camp for the day.

We examined the aerial photograph that purported to show the location of the cache again that night, and with great care. On the morning of the 4th we headed back toward the mountains once more, taking care to follow the indicated bearings, but we spent the whole forenoon in a fruitless search. We could not afford to give any more time to this search so we stopped for our noonday lunch and then began our journey toward the east, keeping close to the foot of the mountains. At 4:30 we were climbing up a fairly steep rise and by 5:30 we found ourselves well up on the foot or the lower end of a great mountain glacier that took its rise on the northern slopes of Mt. Nansen. We stopped to take a look at our surroundings and promptly realized that we had happened upon a very desirable location for our mountain base. Most important of all, the ice clad top of Mt. Nansen was straight ahead of us toward the southwest, and the way to it seemed fairly smooth; furthermore, our location could be approached easily from all sides and appeared to be generally visible from all directions; and lastly the fact that the surface round about was one of loosely compacted snow rather than a hard crusted or sastrugi surface led us to believe that our location was fairly free from strong winds. This was desirable for our own peace of mind and gave us more confidence in our location as a possible landing field, for we did not know but that Commander Byrd might make another flight in this direction.

We called this mountain base, or depot number 8, " Strom Camp," in honor of Sverre Strom, whose work in making sledges for us was perhaps the most important physical contribution made to our success. Without his light flexibly constructed sledges I do not think our journey would have been possible.

On the morning of the 5th while Freddy, Eddie, and Norman were occupied with the task of arranging the camp and taking a careful inventory of all our supplies, Mike, O'Brien, and I drove over toward the east to take a look at what we believed to be Amundsen's Mt. Betty. We had not gone far when a heavy fog came out of nowhere and covered everything with an opaque gray blanket. We were hard put to it to retrace our steps to Strom Camp. We thereupon decided to make no more such jaunts from camp without taking several days' supplies with us or without marking the trail behind us.

The inventory of our supplies was reassuring: especially that of the man food for it showed that we had a little more on hand than we had expected to have; we had not eaten our full rations on the southward journey. The tabulated list showed the following items and amounts:

464 cakes dog food (1 cake 1 ration for 1 dog for 1 day)
 37 bags man pemmican (1 bag 1 day's ration for 6 men)
 33 bags biscuit (1 bag 1 day's ration for 6 men)
 86 lbs. sugar
 65 lbs. of chocolate
 80 lbs. of powdered milk
 50 pounds of oatmeal
 28 pieces of bacon (1 piece 1 day's ration for six men)
100 sausages soup meal
  5 lbs. butter
 16 cans of lemon powder
  6 cans of cocoa
  5 lbs. of tea
  2 lbs. of salt
  6 bags of matches
  6 tin boxes of matches
  8 rolls of toilet paper
  6 lbs. of chipped beef
  1 lb. raisins
  1 small (but large enough) bag of garlic

The last three items were in the way of luxuries beyond the needs of our daily ration; they were most welcome ingredients for variety and for seasoning. Plain pemmican hoosh is a very dull dish.

It will be seen from the above that we had a little more than a full month's supply of man food. We believed that we would be playing safe to use at least three weeks of that supply for field work in the mountains, thus reserving a supply for one week, with which to begin the homeward trek to Little America. Since we expected to reach our depot number 7 within three days at the outside, this seemed a very safe margin.

We had long since decided that our field work should first of all be concentrated upon Mt. Nansen. With this in mind we packed rations for eighteen days on our sledges and on the morning of the 6th started to climb the glacier that lay between us and the exposed slopes of Nansen. Though the snow surface was good for skiing and sledging, it was a hard grind. First of all the lower part of the glacier had a rolling terrain somewhat like that we had found in the lower parts of Liv Glacier, and so for the first few miles we found ourselves climbing up steep slopes just to have to go down again. But the net result was ever upward. We had to be increasingly on our guard for crevasses; they became thicker and more pronounced as we climbed. Fortunately it is relatively easy to avoid them when driving the dogs uphill for the sledges and the teams can be stopped more quickly than under ordinary circumstances.

The dogs were well rested and in spite of the rough travelling we climbed 3000 feet upward over a distance of 15 miles. We made camp under a spur of Mt. Nansen which I thought we would be able to climb easily the next day.

This happened to be the night for our every-other-day radio schedule with Little America. I remember this

"The Mountain Sides were Smoothed and Their Tops Rounded"

night especially on account of the following interesting message from the Commander:

Larry:

Have made most fortunate flight to Marie Byrd Land stop found great mountain range hundred miles east of Scott's Nunatak running north and south stop followed this south for a hundred miles stop mapped it and one hundred fifty miles new coastline to north stop on return flew over Matterhorn stop it is an isolated mountain not very large stop believe this flight of far reaching geographical importance stop by the way am not sure of existence of Carmen Land at least that is of any great size stop mountains run more to eastward than Amundsen indicates don't believe he saw mountains in latitude 84 stop judge this from south polar flight.

Byrd

There was perhaps no sector of the Antarctic where the discovery of new land was of more interest to me than here. I began speculating at once as to whether the aerial photographs taken on the flight would reveal sufficient detail to enable me to decide whether the mountains were like the Andes of South America and the Alps of New Zealand or like our own Queen Maud Mountains.

We got up on the morning of the 7th thinking we had an easy climb ahead of us, but it was the same old story. The rocks were much farther away from us than we had supposed and when we started to climb toward them, we found ourselves barred from a near approach to them by bottomless chasms and crevasses on every side. There was nothing to do but break camp and move on up the glacier; conditions could not be more formidable and they might improve. We drove our teams four miles, increasing our altitude to 4800 feet and then stopped, for there seemed to be no impassable crevasses between us and the rocks at this point. Such places were hard to find for it seemed that nature had outdone herself to keep her geological secrets to herself here in the Queen Maud Mountains. The cover of ice and snow was everywhere so heavy, that patches of bare rock were the exception and not the rule. These were apt to be relatively inaccessible for wherever the slopes were precipitous, the snow and ice had pulled away from the mountain walls leaving great yawning chasms known as " Bergschrunde."

On the morning of the 8th, Mike, Freddy, Eddie, and I put on our skis and roped ourselves together to make our first attempt to reach the rocks. The slopes were steeper and more slippery than we had anticipated and we had to " side hill " or " herring bone " all the way up to a saddle which seemed to be the first stage of our climb. Near the top we had to fairly scramble over a steep ice falls. I doubt if we could have made it without Mike's expert assistance; he was more agile on skis than most people are in ballroom slippers. The crevasses were close together but were fortunately narrow enough so that we dared to cross them with our skis. We had never been able to make this climb with any degree of safety without our skis and even so we got an occasional start as a crevasse roof gave beneath us, but we were saved from falling in because our skis bridged us across.

When we arrived at the saddle we found that we had still to climb about an eighth of a mile to our right along a steep slope with a great yawning chasm only 200 or 300 feet below us. A serious slip and we might have all ended up in it without leaving any trace at all. But we carefully picked our way along the slope and in due time arrived at the coveted rocks.

I had had the unhappy and almost dismal reaction of finding that the higher we climbed, the lower my spirits became, for the nearer we got to the long sought flat-lying rocks, the less they looked like the sedimentary layers I wanted so much to find, and the more they looked like a great series of volcanic flows. And even now, as I review the events of that day I realize that I did not overstate my enthusiasm of the moment when I sent Commander Byrd the following radiogram telling him about the day's work:

No symphony I have ever heard, no work of art before which I have stood in awe ever gave me quite the thrill that I had when I reached out after that strenuous climb and picked up a piece of rock to find it sandstone. It was just the rock I had come all the way to the Antarctic to find.

For I had climbed and clawed my way up over several thousand feet of glacier to the rocks and had actually to hold a piece in my hand before my very eyes, before I realized that it was after all not volcanic rock, but sandstone. That little piece of rock which I first picked up and which was not half as large as the palm of my hand had repaid me for the whole trip. Had it been necessary for me to have turned around that moment and started back to Little America, I should still have felt that it had been a most profitable journey. For this little piece of yellow sandstone, which was a part of the great mass of flat-lying rocks that topped the big mountains like Nansen, told me beyond question that the notions we had formed about these mountains from far out on the shelf ice were correct; that they were simply gigantic blocks of the earth's crust that had been pushed upward into the air 8, 10, or 15 thousand feet. Some of the mountains were higher than the rest for some of the blocks had been pushed up higher. Between some of these massive blocks were great depressions where blocks had been depressed or had sunk. These great rifts or ditches were occupied by mammoth outlet or valley glaciers like Liv and Axel Heiberg which poured down from the plateau into the shelf ice.

Realizing that this was the same kind of sandstone, the same geological formation with the same structure, that Farrar, geologist with Scott's first expedition, had found to characterize the mountains far away on the western borders of the Ross Sea, I knew that our Queen Maud Mountains were but a continuation of those investigated by Farrar, and that the whole was the most stupendous fault block mountain system in all the world.

We became so absorbed in our rock collecting that we did not notice the gathering clouds. Quite suddenly we were completely engulfed. We hastened to snap on our skis and tie fast our ropes thinking that we would be able to see our tracks and retrace our steps. But the snow had been so hard where we had climbed up that we had made scarcely any tracks. Then it began to snow and we all began to get a bit nervous. We started across the slippery slope with the big crevasse that we could not now see, but which we knew was waiting with his mouth open for us, just a few feet below. Only Mike kept his balance throughout; time after time the rest of us slipped and fell, grabbing at the snow as we did so to keep from sliding down the slope. Fortunately we did not all slip at once else Mike could not have held all three of us. We could sort of take turns falling without too greatly endangering the safety of the rest. The snowfall was not great and when we came to the saddle from which the steep slope led down to the level of our camp, we could see our tracks.

After we had crossed the ice falls we knew that there were no dangerous crevasses between us and the bottom of the slope, so we took off our awkward ropes in order that we might descend with greater freedom. Even with all my rocks on his back, Mike slid grandly down to the bottom. Freddy followed him and really did rather well, but it was too steep for persons no more adept at nego-tiating steep slopes than Eddie and I. We tried to follow the examples set by the other two and we slipped and fell and bounced around a good deal and then finally swal-lowed our pride, sat flat down on our skis and disgrace-fully slid to the bottom of the slope.

Eddie Goodale, who proved himself in the course of the summer to have keen eyes, was the first to discover bits of lichens on some of the rocks that we had reached this day. It interested us greatly to realize that this was the farthest south that life of any sort had ever been found.

Though this day had repaid us so richly, we had not been able to climb high enough to get a good cross section of the sandstones we had discovered. We had, however, found that the main great black ribbons running through it, and that had made me think that the whole series might be volcanic in character, were sheets or sills of a dark col-ored igneous rock known as dolerite. This rock had been forced up from the depths in a fluid condition and had pushed its way into the sandstones and spread laterally so uniformly and so widely, that the intrusive sheets that resulted looked as though they might have been formed

right with the sandstones. But we had noted other dark
bands in the yellow sandstones that were clearly not like
these sills. We could not reach any of these rocks from the
location of our first climb so we broke camp on the morning of the 8th and moved six miles farther up the glacier
and, of course, higher than we had been able to drive before. This time we were able to drive our teams much
closer to the rocks, in fact right up under the shadow of
Webster's Peak, which is a spur jutting out from the north
flank of its parent, Mt. Nansen. The slope where we
stopped was so steep that we could find no places flat
enough to pitch our tents on, and we finally had to dig
shelves into the ice and snow to make room for our camp.

The rocks looked so intriguing that this same afternoon
Mike, Norman, Eddie, and I decided to make an ascent.
We climbed up over several hundred feet of granites and
older rocks and found on top of them the same series of
yellow sandstones with the same dark ribbons of volcanic
rock. But we were not satisfied with this discovery, so on
we went, higher and higher with the slopes getting steeper
all the way. Finally Mike and I were climbing up over ice
walls so steep that I had to chop steps with my ice axe to
keep on going. Then up over ragged and pinnacled col-
umns of the dark volcanic rocks. Mike outstripped me and
soon brought back to me little bits of rock from the darker
bands that we were trying to reach. Though with some reluctance, these burned when a lighted match was held to
them — they were a low grade of coal. Thus we had discovered coal little more than 300 miles from the South
Pole.

I had anticipated this discovery as soon as I realized that
the sandstone formation was identical with that found by

The Midnight Sun In The Antarctic

Farrar, for the "Beacon Sandstone," as he called this formation, had been found to contain coal in several different localities. But our finding of the coal seams here so greatly extends the known coal bearing areas in this extensive sandstone formation, that it is at once evident that David, who was geologist with Shackleton's first expedition, was not over enthusiastic in his estimate that there was in the Antarctic a coal field covering fully 100,000 square miles. As Griffith Taylor [1] has pointed out, Antarctica may well have the most extensive coal reserves in all the world with the possible single exception of the United States.

Because Antarctica is still locked in the grip of an ice age, it surprises many people to know that it has not always been so. In fact glacial conditions such as exist now seem to be the exception rather than the rule. Coal is one of a number of evidences that it once had a climate that was temperate to sub-tropical at least. In the record of the rocks that we know, there is no evidence that glacial conditions existed in the Antarctic until the coming of the great Ice Age, in very recent geological time, which still holds sway over this continent. For millions of years before this, it had a climate more nearly uniform with the rest of the world.

On our climb up and beyond Webster's Peak we had crossed a vertical thickness of 2000 feet of the Beacon Sandstone. Our rough measurements demonstrated that the whole formation attains a thickness of at least 7000 feet on Mt. Nansen. We wanted to continue our climb clear to the summit of this great mountain but the slopes above rose in an almost vertical wall so that there was no possibil-

---

[1] Taylor, Griffith. *Antarctic Adventure and Research*, Appleton, 1930, pp. 100–101.

ity of doing it here. But we were unwilling to give up hope yet, so we broke camp and sledged back to the scene of our first climb. We thought we might be able to cross the saddle which had been the first stage of our climb up this side and find a route on the other side of it by which we might be able to reach the top.

There was nothing for me to gain by climbing up this saddle again so I sent Mike, Norman, and O'Brien up to look the situation over. Freddy and Eddie expected to join me in an attack upon some rocks lower down that I had not yet examined. Our approach to the rocks was completely barred by great crevasses so we returned to camp to await the report from the other three. Their report was unfavorable so we decided to sledge back down the glacier to Strom Camp and then head eastward along the foot of the range. If when we came to the mouth of Axel Heiberg Glacier it seemed feasible to climb Mt. Nansen from this approach, we planned to attempt it.

Though going down the glacier was much easier on the dogs than the ascent had been, it was none the less fraught with considerably greater hazards on account of the much greater difficulty of controlling the teams and the sledges. It was almost impossible to stop the dogs quickly and within a short space when we were going down a steep slope. We went a large part of the way with the sledges " rough locked," that is we wound heavy ropes around the runners so they would drag more heavily and not slide headlong onto the dogs when the slopes became especially steep.

The climb up the glacier had been over such a rough route that we thought we could go down more smoothly and with greater safety, if we did not retrace our steps but

rather went out into the middle. There were fewer crevasses there and the whole surface appeared to be smoother
than along the eastern side where we had come up. We
were slipping merrily along when a curious feeling came
over us that things were not quite right. We could not see
a single thing to cause us any alarm, but we stopped and
retraced our steps so that we could go down a more gentle
slope, which we could see all the way to its bottom or
break. As we slid down this slope, we looked back and
found that we had turned about and retraced our steps
from almost the edge of a great ice cliff fully 100 feet high.
We smiled at our good fortune and continued on our way.

If one wants sledging thrills that sometimes approach the
nerve racking, he can get them more closely packed into a
shorter space of time by trying to manipulate dog teams
down the steep slopes of a crevassed glacier than any other
way I know of. We had found one place, especially, on our
way up that might be critical, and that was a place where
the glacier narrowed up and crevasses shot out from either
side of the valley, leaving sort of a gateway of safety between. We concentrated upon the problem of guiding the
dogs so as to hit this gap. Fortunately the glacier flattened
out before we reached it and we were able to slow down
and find our way through.

We were most desirous of locating Mt. Betty before we
started on the eastward leg of our journey. We had not yet
been able to orient ourselves with reference to Amundsen's
chart, but we felt that if we could be sure of the identity of
a single peak, we could relate the other features to it. In
his account of the journey home from the South Pole
Amundsen makes the following statement about his stop
at Mt. Betty:

At the same time we built a great cairn, and left there a can of 17 liters of paraffin, 2 packets of matches — containing 20 boxes — and an account of our expedition. Possibly someone may find a use for these things in the future.

This relatively small rock mass was the only one Amundsen and his party had climbed, and this cairn was the only record they had left anywhere on the rocks in their whole long trek. To find this cairn, which would identify Mt. Betty, was our only hope of definitely tying up our work with his and of being able to interpret his identification of the various features shown on his chart. Accordingly we decided that when we came down the glacier, we would turn to the right, and sledge over to the peak which we believed to be Mt. Betty, before returning to Strom Camp. This was the same low peak that Mike, O'Brien, and I had started out to examine on the 5th when we were caught in the fog.

Just at noon we arrived at the foot of the desired mountain where we stopped for lunch before proceeding with our investigation. This was the first place in all of our travels about the mountains where we had been able to drive our dogs right up to the rocks. These were the first rocks that the young dogs, born in Little America, had ever seen. It was a new experience to them. They shied away from them at first and then approached very gingerly, sniffing eagerly for some familiar odor. Finally Bob screwed up his courage enough to lick the rock. Finding that he could neither bite it nor be bitten by it, he immediately lost interest.

After our brief lunch we tethered the dogs and prepared to climb the mountain to look for the cairn. It was only a little step from where we had to leave our dogs to the top yet the barometer showed an altitude at the top of 2600 feet above sea level whereas Amundsen had given the height of his Mt. Betty as 1200 feet. Nevertheless there was no other mountain or rock mass that could possibly fit his location so we made a thorough search. There was nothing to be seen that even remotely resembled a cairn. Much disappointed we turned our steps back toward our base camp.

We awoke on the morning of the 11th in Strom Camp to find the wind blowing a half gale and the snow beginning to weave its way down the slopes about us. We dared not think of travelling in such poor visibility. We had learned that sledging about these mountains and glaciers with their many crevasses was, even under the best conditions, a sufficiently hazardous occupation. To attempt to travel without being able to see well would have been to invite disaster a little bit too openly. There was nothing for us to do but remain in camp.

The wind lulled toward the end of the day and it looked as though we should be able to travel again on the 12th. We were not a little amazed when we had finished our supper to look out of the cook tent and see a skua gull feeding on bits of dog food just a few feet away from us. We could scarcely believe our eyes, for we knew that the nearest water to us was north of Little America and that normally these gulls get their food from the open sea. Just why this solitary bird had flown some 500 miles in as direct a line as he could have taken away from his native habitat was quite beyond our understanding. There seemed to be no reason and less instinct about it. The thought of any kind of fresh meat, even that of the skua gull whose appetite we knew to be as varied and as depraved as that of a goat, was tempting.

We discussed the advisability of killing our visitor and having a stew, but the thought of his untidy ways of getting a living were too much for us. We preferred to continue with the drab monotony of our pemmican so we allowed the gull to eat his fill of dog food and go on his way.

Eager as we were to be off toward the east, we had about decided that it was worth while to make one more attempt to locate the airplane cache of food and fuel. Our plans were all made so as not to make any use of these supplies, but in case of the loss of one of our sledges down a crevasse, it would be a satisfying thing indeed to know just where there were 200 pounds of additional supplies within reach.

I had radioed Commander Byrd about our inability to locate the depot from the marked airplane photograph and he had given me further detailed instructions which I thought would enable us to locate it. On the morning of the 12th Eddie Goodale and I set forth with his team to make one last search. We sledged 34 miles and found the cache with but little difficulty. We discovered that its location had been marked on the wrong photograph and that it was in a slight depression which made it difficult to be seen from the surface. In fact we had driven our dogs to within 300 yards of it before we saw it.

We loaded the 200 pounds of food and 5 gallons of gasoline onto our sledge and drove back to Strom Camp. The knowledge that we had so great a surplus of man food gave us a very great additional safety factor as we completed our preparations to start eastward on the 13th.

CHAPTER VIII

EASTWARD TO MARIE BYRD LAND

Only the Air-spirits know
What lies beyond the hills,
Yet I urge my team farther on
Drive on and on,
On and on!
Eskimo song as translated by KNUD RASMUSSEN

THOUGH the next day was Friday and was also the 13th we did not delay our plans to get started eastward. After a morning spent in lashing three weeks supplies onto our sledges and building a huge snow beacon around the cache of supplies we were leaving at Strom Camp, we headed toward the east into lands unknown and unexplored. The sun was bright overhead and 20 miles off to our right, except for a few strands of fleecy clouds, mighty Mt. Fridtjof Nansen was silhouetted against the clear deep blue of the sky; but, curiously enough, the shelf ice off to our left was covered with low-lying clouds that completely hid everything from view. As we looked across the tops of these clouds we could easily fancy ourselves sledging along the shores of a great sea.

The dogs were unusually full of life after their day of rest, and we spent the early part of the day's run in untangling them and getting started right. As we were sliding down a slope beyond the mountain which we had believed to be Mt. Betty, we found the gradient getting much steeper than we had anticipated. It was too late to attempt to stop the dogs and rough lock the sledges, so on we went, hoping that the teams would keep clear of each other. I was sliding grandly along on my skis with Vaughan's team on one side of me and Goodale's on the other. Suddenly without sufficient warning to enable me to change my course, the two teams began to converge and gathered speed as they did so. There was no stopping them and I became a bit too excited to stop myself, even by my usual emergency method of sitting down, and just as the two teams came together into one grand fight I landed in their midst. The hair began to fly and purely from the standpoint of self preservation, I threshed around with all my might with my skis and my ski sticks. In my attempts to extricate myself without getting chewed up I incidentally stopped the dog fight. I was never very adept as a dog driver and I have not yet confessed to Vaughan and Goodale that I did not purposely slide into the dogs to stop the fight.

With 19 miles behind us we stopped for the night on the western side of the lower slopes of Axel Heiberg Glacier. Though we had failed definitely to locate Mt. Betty there could be no question but that we were on the margin of the great glacier up which Amundsen had driven his dogs when he was bound for the South Pole eighteen years before us. No camp of our whole journey was in a more complete fairyland setting. Across the glacier from us the ice clad peak of Mt. Don Pedro Christopherson pierced the clouds that hid his lower slopes; above us was Mt. Nansen completely covered with ice and snow on this side, and off to the south the sun was flooding with pure gold, the great gap between these two mountains that is filled with the ice stream of Axel Heiberg Glacier; and behind it all an apple green sky that one can see only over great areas of ice, such as stretched away toward the south beyond the mountains.

When we awoke on the morning of the 14th, we found the sky completely overcast and the air calm and dead. Soon great soft flakes of snow began to fall. There was no visibility; we seemed suspended in a world of white. Whichever way one looked, whether up, down, to the right or to the left, or ahead, there was only the tenuous wall of opaque white. We had skirted some great crevasses to reach the spot where we were camped and knew that the glacial ice across which we had to travel would be badly broken up. It was unsafe to venture beyond the known limits of our camping place; there was nothing to do but sit tight. We remained in our tents and slept most of the day. Meantime the snow was piling up all about us and by night some eight inches had fallen, but in the late evening the clouds began to get thinner and we disposed of our evening hoosh and crawled into our sleeping bags with high hopes that we should be under way with the morning.

The white gloom was thicker than ever on the morning of the 15th and it was still snowing. It was a soft wet snow that partially melted on everything that it happened to fall upon. The temperature went up to the unheard of height of 35 degrees above zero. The dogs were restless and miserable for they do not like wetness. Water was dripping from the tops and sides of our tents for they were not waterproof and we could not keep them free of snow and our sleeping bags were beginning to get clammy. Of course our equipment was not waterproof, and it seemed as though everything would get soggy before we could break camp and dry out.

Before the day ended we were beginning to sense one very real kind of monotony in sledging. We had no place to go and we were wet and cold and much more uncomfortable than we had been with the temperature 50 degrees colder. We grew so chilly that we found it difficult to sit still and do nothing. Then somebody dug out a deck of cards which proved to be something in the way of a godsend. We rolled up our sleeping bags so as not to get them any wetter and sat around for the rest of the day on the wet tent floor playing hearts, with our daily ration of chocolate for stakes. It was a great relief. When we left Little America each man had been allowed to bring one book along for just such emergencies of monotony as this, but everyone had left his book at Strom Camp.

The decreasing activity seemed to have no effect on the appetites of either the dogs or the men. The rations were disappearing and correspondingly shortening our possible exploration of Carmen Land.

For the first time since we had left Little America we had snow soft enough and wet enough so that we could wash in it, but unfortunately nobody had thought to bring any soap. Without it we rubbed and scrubbed in vain to remove the ravages of the " Antarctic disease."

The morning of the 16th came without bringing us any hope. It was still a milky opaque world and still it snowed. We got up to find our tents sagging under their weight of snow, like evergreens sag under such loads back home. The dogs were living in wells or pits for as they lay curled up, the snow had accumulated so thickly around them that they were completely obscured from one's view as he looked

THE END OF THE TREK
CAIRN ON SUPPORTING PARTY MOUNTAIN

We built a huge Cairn a few feet from the Amundsen Cairn (lower right)

across toward them from the tents. Conditions were getting well-nigh intolerable, but in the early afternoon it ceased snowing and the visibility began to get better. By 11 o'clock that night the clouds were actually breaking away and we crawled into our bags for what we hoped would be our last Turkish bath-like sleep. And it was the last.

We awoke on the 17th to a brilliant sunny day and began the task of recovering our supplies and equipment from beneath their blanket of snow. It was mid-forenoon before we could get started and then we found that the sledges pulled so hard through the 18 inches of soft snow that it was necessary for us to break some sort of trail for the dogs. I followed behind Mike on my skis, making a path or track through the deep snow beside the one made by him and the dogs were then able to manage the sledges along this rude roadway.

At 10:30 we stopped, ostensibly to make some observations, but more particularly I believe because we could not take our eyes off the view we were leaving behind. We were right in the middle of the lower reaches of Axel Heiberg Glacier. On the left was Mt. Don Pedro Christopherson looking like a great elongated pyramid of solid ice and snow with his long gable ridged top. Not the tiniest wisp of cloud marred the perfection of his silhouette against the bright sky. To the right the great tabular topped Mt. Nansen so completely smothered with ice and snow that not the merest patch of bare rock was exposed and looking for all the world like a great Greek temple of whitest marble. We could not help remarking on what a perfect monument it was to the man for whom it was named, for Amundsen had called it in honor of his countryman

Fridtjof Nansen, and as befitted a name than which none stands higher on the roll of honor in polar exploration, it was lofty and beautiful and dignified and strong. Stretching down between these mighty mountains was the great glacier which Amundsen had traversed twice during his polar journey and down which Commander Byrd and his polar party had flown when they were homeward bound. Near the head or top of the glacier we could see the " toppling crags " of a great ice falls which we would have to cross if we expected to reach the top of Mt. Nansen from the plateau behind. This would be fraught with certain hazard and would consume so much of our time that we would not be able to make our eastward journey to Carmen Land. We were unanimous in our decision that our most profitable course was to proceed eastward along the foot of the range without attempting to scale the heights of Mt. Nansen.

We built a large snow beacon at this mid-point of Axel Heiberg Glacier which we called Ipswich Beacon and which was to serve as an essential control point in the surveys Mike was carrying on. We then continued on our way, hoping to be able to stay fairly close to the foothills, both to avoid the clouds that seemed so much more prevalent over the shelf ice than they were over the mountains, and, to make as frequent examinations of the exposed rocks as possible. We had not gone far when we realized that such a course was quite impossible. Directly ahead of us along the eastern margins of Axel Heiberg Glacier, the ice was so heavily crevassed and broken up that it would have been little short of suicide to have attempted to cross over. We had no other course but to head northward out onto the shelf ice until we were beyond the worst of the crevassed zone and then alter our course to parallel the foot of the mountains.

In spite of the heavy travelling the dogs were in unusually good form. We had learned that there were two very easy ways by which we could tell the condition of our huskies. When they were feeling fit and ready for work their tails were curled over their backs and if they had proper " husky " ears they would be pointed ahead at attention; as they grew tired their tails drooped until in their supreme dejection they trailed along between their legs. Again we found that the measure of our difficulties in getting started on a new day's travel was something of a guide to the condition of the dogs. In proportion as they were full of pent up energy they were eager to be off and in like proportion were hard to manage. The three days of idleness when we were snow-bound had given all our dogs renewed energy, and it seemed we had to be forever stopping to untangle them on this morning, of all times, when we were so eager to cover the miles in a hurry.

We were pushing our way along through the snow down the lower slopes of Axel Heiberg Glacier when I heard Mike call. I looked up to see him pointing off to the left of the trail with his ski stick. There to the left and still ahead of me was what appeared to be a good sized field, covered with puff balls of snow! This turned out to be about the most freakish phenomenon we saw all summer. Here was a patch of snow about two hundred yards wide and a quarter of a mile long strewn with spherical puffs of snow from the size of one's fist to that of a basket ball. From a distance they looked like balls of snow that had grown by accretion about a nucleus as they had been rolled along the surface by the wind, in other words they seemed to have been formed in quite the same way that youngsters in our home latitudes make snowballs by rolling them through soft wet snow. A closer examination showed that these spheres were indeed puffs; the snow of which they were formed did not seem to be the least bit compacted. They had no appreciable weight and one could not pick them up without having them fall into a million pieces in his hands and still have nothing left! Furthermore they were generally hollow. Could one imagine a ball of air rolling over the surface and attracting to itself enough loose snow to form these spheres he would have a good notion of just how they looked to us. Light, fluffy and unpacked as they were, I can think of no way by which these " puff balls " could have been formed except by some such rolling accretion. Their distribution was so localized that conditions for their formation must be very exacting. In all of our travels we never saw this phenomenon repeated.

As we headed outward from the mountains and away from Axel Heiberg Glacier, we turned to look up a big outlet glacier just east of Mt. Don Pedro Christopherson that was the most perfect one we had yet seen. Sheer clean cut walls bounded it on either side, and it stretched away toward the south in one grand sweep that so far as we could see was unbroken by such great ice falls as we had noted toward the heads of Liv and Axel Heiberg Glaciers.

By the time we had cleared the worst of the crevassed region we had sledged 15 miles and the surplus energy with which the dogs had begun the day was largely exhausted, so we made camp for the night. The cloud cover that had been hanging low over the shelf ice soon descended and we found ourselves under a blanket of cloud-fog.

But it was bright, and the world was sparkling all about us when I wormed myself out of my bag on the morning of the 18th; the mists were all gone. We were shortly on our way headed almost due east. As our morning lengthened into day we could see a great hole opening in the mountain scarp to our right. By midday we were looking up the most stupendous glacier that we had yet seen. It was larger than either of the two great outlet glaciers (Liv and Axel Heiberg) that Amundsen had discovered and named, and was quite the grandest unnamed feature we had yet seen, and, pending Commander Byrd's approval, I called it for the man who had discovered the Queen Maud Mountains "Amundsen Glacier."

Marking the boundary of this great ice stream on the east were three neighboring and friendly peaks that towered above those around them. These will be Mounts Crockett, Vaughan, and Goodale.

We found the travelling immensely easier this day for we had gotten well beyond the soft snow and slid along toward Carmen Land making good time. For be it said that although we had long ago had grave doubts cast into our minds as to the actual existence of this highland, we were not entirely sure as yet that it did not exist. There were blue-black cloud peaks along our eastern horizon on this very day that caused some differences of opinion among us as to whether they were really mountains or clouds. We were not sure until we drew nearer to them that they were clouds. The fact that our studies at this time and later on were to completely change the geography of this part of the Antarctic as Amundsen believed it to be is no reflection

on his work. Not even in the desert does one find more
puzzling and contradictory phenomena than abound in the
brilliantly clear air of the Antarctic. Fantastic mirages and
overheightened mountains and ridges due to looming were
common occurrences.

In the middle of the afternoon on the 18th we found
ourselves getting into the fringes of a great ice field. Again
we headed outward onto the shelf ice thinking we might be
able to go around the ice. But it only grew worse and the
surface so slippery that we had to hang onto the sledges
to keep from falling for we could no longer manage our
skis. Finally we decided to turn abruptly to our right and
head in to the foot of the mountains and then climb to a
top where we could get a good look off toward the north
and east. We hoped to be able to see a way around this
great field of glare ice that was blocking our eastward
progress.

As we neared the mountains I was struck by the great
difference between their outlines and those about Liv and
Axel Heiberg Glaciers. To the west we had found the front
peaks to be ragged and angular, but here the mountain
sides were smoothed and their tops were rounded as though
a mighty giant had planed and polished them all. Such
forms result only from the grinding action beneath great
thicknesses of ice. It was the most positive kind of evidence
that here at least, the ice must once have been thicker than
it is now. In fact as we climbed higher and looked about
us, we had the impression that it must at one time have
been so thick that it flowed down over these parts in such
great floods that few peaks were exposed above it. Rough
measurements of the heights of the peaks hereabouts suggested the reason. Eastward from the great mountain

masses that border Axel Heiberg Glacier the general altitude of the whole range had become lower. In the vicinity
of these glaciers such great masses as Mt. Nansen, Don
Pedro Christopherson, and Ruth Gade had been high
enough, even when the ice on the plateau behind was at its
thickest, to stem its unbridled flow down onto the shelf
ice, hence many of the front peaks had not been rounded
off beneath the ice as they had been here to the east of
Amundsen Glacier.

We had one of the greatest surprises of the summer at
the camp which we established at the foot of one of these
rounded glacial tops. We could very distinctly hear the
gurgle of running water. This seemed strange for the air
temperature had not been above freezing, but we could
not mistake our ears — there is no other sound in all the
world like that of rapid water. Shortly we found an ice
clad brook which owed its existence to the thaw water
formed where the snow and ice adjoined the rocks, for
even though the air may have rarely if ever risen to a
thawing temperature here, it was evident that the rocks
on the northern slopes did absorb enough heat from the
sun to raise their own temperatures well above freezing
and hence melt any snow or ice that happened to be near
them. This thaw water brooklet grew colder as it descended the icy mountain side and its mouth emptied into
a lake of blue ice. It was a novel sight to watch this stream
of liquid water emptying into and becoming at once a
part of this lake of ice, for even as the water from the
brook spread out over the ice of the lake, it appeared to
simultaneously reach the freezing temperature and become
one with the ice lake.

What we had suspected about the trend of the front of

the Queen Maud Mountains was verified when we were able to check our dead reckoning position here with an astronomical observation on the sun. We found that the range did not trend southeastward from the vicinity of Axel Heiberg Glacier as Amundsen thought but that rather it is continued in an almost due easterly direction from it. Furthermore we looked away toward the east and north for signs of Carmen Land. There were none. We were now sure beyond any shadow of doubt that it did not exist.

Our climb over the rocks in this vicinity yielded one novelty, in that we found the first evidence of any metallic mineralization that had yet been discovered in the Queen Maud Mountains. We found some scant surface showings of copper but nothing to indicate any great deposit. But it was a welcome variety from the dark colored old metamorphic rocks which was all we found anywhere except up the higher slopes of Mt. Nansen.

For the new information that we had gotten about the mountains this camp had been an abundantly interesting place, but when we looked off toward the east and north from the mountain tops about it, the prospect of finding an easy way to skirt the great ice field that had caused us to turn in to the mountains at this point was rather dismal. We could not see the limits of it, but our best bet seemed to be to sledge northward for at least ten miles before we attempted to head further eastward. With these intentions in mind we left our camp on the morning of the 19th. We had gone but a few miles when we found ourselves in the midst of a glare ice field that reached beyond our horizon both to the east and to the north. To go ahead as we had planned was most certainly fraught with some uncertainty but even though we had satisfied all our doubts as to the non-existence of Carmen Land, we did not want to turn back yet. Not only did we want to carry our geological and geographical studies as far eastward as possible and for this reason alone did not want to turn back, but there was an additional reason why we wanted to sledge beyond the 150th meridian.

More than 500 miles north of us Commander Byrd had skirted the coast of the continent beyond this meridian which marked the eastern boundary of British claims. The new lands which he had discovered to the east of this meridian he had claimed for the United States, and had named in honor of his wife Marie Byrd Land. But no one had ever set foot on this American claimed Antarctic Land, and, there was the question that a claim based solely on the fact of a flight over a new land might be questioned since it was without precedent. We were therefore very anxious to back up Commander Byrd's claims by sledging to the east of this boundary meridian and be the first persons to actually set foot on land within the American claimed sector.

We had a good supply of food and the dogs were in fine condition so we decided to risk the crossing of the ice fields. But the ice grew worse as we progressed and like our approach through the crevasses at the foot of Liv Glacier conditions became so bad that we couldn't decide whether it was safer to carry on or attempt to retrace our steps, and so of course we kept on our way. A mile or two within the margin of this ice field, the surface had become so slippery that we had to take off our skies and ride on the sledges. Crevasses were numerous but fortunately they were short and for the most part partially filled with snow, so that they stood out in sharp contrast to the wind swept ice about them. We could always see them easily enough but seeing them and avoiding them were quite different matters. As usual the dogs were pretty smart about keeping themselves out of the crevasses, but after they had crossed one in safety, or had avoided it, they cared little about what happened to the sledges they were dragging behind them. In spite of all of our efforts we were forever crashing onto the roofs of these crevasses and then holding our breath until we knew whether they were going to hold or not, until the sledge had crossed over. They didn't always hold; there were a good many spills but the crevasses were not so wide but that we escaped any very deep falls. Nevertheless getting over or around them was much like a game of tag.

We became so absorbed with our game of getting across the ice with its crevasses that we did not watch the changing façade of the mountain front on our right as carefully as we usually did. I don't think any of us realized until we had stopped to make camp for the day that directly south of us was another great gap in the mountain wall, fully as wide as that through which Amundsen Glacier pushes its floods of ice. This great portal was more clear cut and straighter than any we had previously seen. There seemed to be literally nothing between us and the South Pole through this gateway. For him who charted the outlines of this mammoth stream of ice and who did all of the topographical work for the geological party this is Thorne Glacier.

My feelings were a mixture of curiosity and very real awe, as I looked up this new glacier and across the mountains to the east, knowing that ours were the first human eyes ever to look upon them. It falls to the lot of few men any more to thus view parts of the earth for the first time.

And we knew in very truth that we were the first, for not even had primitive man ever existed on the Antarctic Continent, and civilized man had not been this way before.

We had maintained radio communication with Little America on alternate days throughout our journey and on the night of the 19th, Freddy, as usual, was able to make good contact. I remember this day especially for we received the good news that Commander Byrd had been made a Rear Admiral by special act of congress.

The ice still stretched away from us in all directions as we started out on the morning of the 20th. It was the same old game of tag that we had played on the previous day. Fortunately neither we nor the dogs were hurt as we went bouncing along into and over, or out of the crevasses, but the sledges took " an awful beating." Both runners of one of our very finest sledges, a Strom-Balchen sledge, were splintered, and runners on two of the three remaining sledges we were using were cracked. We knew that if this kept up much longer we should have great difficulty even in getting back to Strom Camp. Afternoon came and though the sledges, in spite of the additional load of our weight, hauled easily on the glare ice it was hard for the dogs to keep their footing, and they were constantly being jerked about as the sledges skidded. It was all very wearing on them and we wanted to make camp early, but we could find no place where we could erect our tents and stake out the dogs and so we kept on going. Farther eastward the icy surface gave way in places to a hard almost flinty snow surface and the rolling surface of the shelf ice became more pronounced. I mean that the rolls into which the shelf ice is pushed by the glacial streams through the mountains became more pronounced. These rolls were transverse to the mountain front even as similar ones had been below Liv Glacier. Their forward slopes were steeper and more broken or crevassed than the back or mountainward facing slope. Ahead of us we could see a great gap in the mountain wall that looked from our distant view to be wide enough to accommodate a glacier far larger than any we had yet seen. We steered our courses to fetch up with the eastern margin of this huge glacier, and in the very late evening we reached a nunatak near its mouth where we found a patch of snow on which we could make our camp. It had been a frightfully hard day for the dogs, for we had come 29 miles since morning.

Our dead reckoning position indicated that we had come well to the eastward of the 150th meridian, that we were within the sector of lands claimed by Admiral Byrd. When the others had turned in for the night I got some sun observations which told me that our camp, which we had decided to call Camp Coman for the surgeon of the expedition, was located at latitude 85 degrees and 25 minutes south and longitude 147 degrees and 55 minutes west. We had arrived; and this turned out to be both our farthest east and farthest south point.

Over our oatmeal the next morning we discussed the problem of just what to do, now that we were actually about to set foot upon the rocks. We had only a tiny American flag with us but we fastened it to a thin piece of bamboo and then walked up to the nearest rocks and planted our flag. We took off our hats and stood at attention for a moment of awkward silence until I said:

" Put your hats on! "

Thus ended our notion of the proper ceremony for laying claim to new lands. We then cast lots to see who would have to remain in camp with the dogs and Freddy lost. Not since we had left Little America had we ever ventured more than a few feet from camp without leaving someone to watch the dogs. We dared not take any chances of losing any through fighting way out here.

The rest of us climbed to the top of the highest peak which was accessible from our camp, and which we named Supporting Party Mountain in honor of the group whose preliminary work had made possible this extended journey of ours. Here we built a cairn of rocks inside of which I left a small tin can with a tight cover. Inside the tin can is a page from my notebook on which is given a brief account of the journey of the geological party and the statement that we "in the name of Admiral Richard Evelyn Byrd claim this land as a part of Marie Byrd Land, a dependency or possession of the United States of America." We realized that the rocks upon which we stood might have no connection with the lands seen by Commander Byrd on his flight into Marie Byrd Land, in other words that this might be a separate land; nevertheless we were within the sector claimed by him, and we elected to extend the name he had given, to include the portion we had explored.

Though we found that the general level of the mountains was even lower here than where we had climbed up between Amundsen and Thorne Glaciers, their character was unchanged. Here we found the same fore peaks of old, old rocks that had formed the foothills of the mountains throughout the whole of our trek. Here they were smoothed and polished by glacial action as we had found them to be between Thorne and Amundsen Glaciers. Many miles farther back in the plateau we could see the tabular masses which we assumed to be similar to Mt. Nansen.

Throughout the whole of our eastward journey from Axel Heiberg Glacier we had found the Queen Maud Mountains getting ever progressively lower and the covering of ice and snow so much thicker that we could not help speculating upon the possibility of the range disappearing completely beneath the ice farther to the east. As I looked toward the south and east from the top of Supporting Party Mountain I had the unmistakable impression that the mountains now exposed in these directions may have been completely overridden by the ice during a period when it was surely much thicker than now. Even now it seemed that the mountains were almost drowned by the glacial ice, for it was pushing out into the shelf ice here in much greater volume than at any other place we had observed.

My own interest was principally absorbed by the great glacier that flowed out into the shelf ice in an almost westerly direction between our Supporting Party Mountain and what appeared to be the main fault scarp of the mountains. For one who was an inspiring teacher to me in my first studies in geology, and who is now beyond his three score years and ten, and who devoted his life to the study of glaciation with results too far-reaching ever to be evaluated, this glacier is named the Leverett Glacier. We could not see the head of this huge ice stream, but its mouth is wider than that of any glacier we had seen in our whole trek and the volume of ice that it was adding to the shelf ice was immeasurably greater than that Liv or Amundsen or any other was bringing down from the plateau.

The longest known glacier in the world is Beardmore which flows down through the fault block mountain rim of the Ross Sea depression some 175 miles west of Axel Heiberg Glacier. It is 130 miles long. The map of the Queen Maud Mountains as compiled by the American Geographical Society from data brought back both by the geological party and the south polar flight party indicates that Amundsen Glacier is 100 miles long and that Thorne Glacier is 90 miles long. There are no other glaciers except Beardmore known to be as long as these, hence *Amundsen becomes the second and Thorne the third longest glaciers known.* Yet neither of these glaciers and probably no other glacier except Beardmore contributes so much glacial ice to the Ross Shelf Ice as does Leverett Glacier, and I suspect that when it is mapped in its entirety we shall find that *it is longer than either Amundsen or Thorne Glaciers.*

My mind was filled with many questions as I took a last look eastward from the top of Supporting Party Mountain: do the Queen Maud Mountains further flatten out to the east to lose their identity beneath the continental ice cap? Do they continue across the continent to the Weddell Sea, perhaps to form a boundary of it? Do they swing toward the north to connect somewhere with the Edsel Ford Mountains and thus form the eastern boundary of the Ross Sea Depression? Should we be able to answer any of these questions if we continued a few miles farther to the east, and thus throw a vast new amount of light upon the question of the possible connection of the Ross and Weddell Seas?

Though I cannot yet prove it conclusively, there is little doubt in my mind about this whole question. *I do not think the two seas are in any way connected;* I think their position opposite each other is accidental. Though the aerial photographs of the Edsel Ford Mountains were taken from too great a distance to reveal any details of the mountains, they, nevertheless, appear to me to be quite an exact counterpart of the Queen Maud Mountains; in other words they appear to be *fault block mountains bounding a great plateau*. Like the Queen Maud Mountains they have a *straight clear cut front and at least one great outlet glacier* can be distinguished in the photographs. It seems more reasonable to assume that this plateau *is connected with the South Polar Plateau than that it is entirely independent of it*. Lastly the position of Leverett Glacier suggests a source through some great mountain wall to the east, running in a general north-south direction.

I have suggested on the general map opposite page 124 my notions as to the relationships described above. In the insert on the large map of the Queen Maud Mountains opposite page 193 is given the suggestive connection between the Ross and Weddell Seas, which I believe is no longer tenable. Of course there may be a depression between the South Polar Plateau and the Marie Byrd Land Plateau, but I think the structural affinities are very real.

I believe that had we been able to sledge fifty to one hundred miles, or perhaps even less, farther east we should have demonstrated the actuality of the relationships, that I have briefly indicated above as being possible. To turn my back on all this and head back toward Strom Camp was one of the very real " hardships " of the expedition. But it would have been sheer foolhardiness to have gone on. Our supplies were limited, especially the dog food, and we knew that the dogs could not endure much more of the sort of work that they had been subjected to during their last two days of travel. Ahead the surface was icy and crevassed and all that we crossed would have to be recrossed, and already there lay a forty mile expanse of such

THE AMUNDSEN CAIRN ON MT. BETTY

6 - 7 janr. 1912.

Nådde å inncirklet polen
14de - 16de decembr. 1911.

Bestemte Victoria land s a - samt
synteris - Kong Edward VII Land's Sa..
mensætning ved 86° S. Br, samt disse
landes fortsættelse i en mektig fjeld -
kjede mot SO. Har iaktatt denne
kjedes utstrækning till 88° S. Br. Samt
synteris - efter leiften å dømme - strækker
sig sen videre i samme retning over
det antarktiske kontinent. - Passerte dette
sted på tilbakeveien ine forsvyne fem 60 dage,
2 slur, 11 kummr. Allt velt.
Roal Amundsen

sledging between us and Strom Camp. There was no way but to head along the foot of the mountains.

We planned to travel by night when we started back toward Strom Camp, for we should in this way have the sun more nearly behind our backs. Though the sun was always well above the horizon as it completed its circle overhead every twenty-four hours, we had found it much harder on our eyes to travel toward it than away from it, for the reflected glare from the snow as we faced into the sun was intense and very tiring to the eyes. We got badly confused with our time and our dates until we became accustomed to the idea of the date changing at our " noon-time " instead of while we slept; but it was necessary that we keep our dates straight, both for the sake of our regular radio schedules with Little America and for purposes of navigation.

Recrossing the ice fields proved to be just as great a nightmare as had been the original crossing. The wear and tear was telling on the sledges. We had to abandon one Strom-Balchen sledge for its runners had been completely splintered, and the runners of the other one were cracked. These had been such good sledges to handle that we had loaded them too heavily and had worked them too hard. How they had stood up so long was something of a miracle, yet they would have stood all this buffeting about and much more if their makers could have gotten the right kind of materials for runners, but hickory of the right thickness was not to be had in Little America.

This recrossing of the crevassed glare ice took heavy toll on the dogs' strength too. Many played out completely and had to be taken out of harness; even old Targish, who was one of the hardiest creatures I have ever seen, grew so weak that he had to be allowed to run loose. Some were limping, for the ice had been hard on their feet and several showed a disinclination to eat their daily ration of pemmican when we stopped to make camp. This had never happened before. We were all glad that we had not decided to sledge eastward from Supporting Party Mountain.

It was with the greatest relief that we saw the last of the slick ice. For the rest of the way back to Strom Camp we should have a good snow surface for we expected to retrace our steps, so that we could stop at Ipswich Beacon to make some further observations to check those we made when we built the beacon on our way eastward.

CHAPTER IX

THE AMUNDSEN CAIRN

And here on snows, where never human foot
Of common mortal trod, we nightly tread,
And leave no trace; o'er the savage sea,
The glassy ocean of the mountain ice,
We skim its rugged breakers, which put on
The aspect of a tumbling tempest's foam,
Frozen in a moment — a dead whirlpool's image.

BYRON

WE were glad to be headed back toward the mountains
along our former trail on the afternoon of the 23rd,
for there before us was the prospect that had so delighted
us as we were leaving Ipswich Beacon to head eastward.
The whole world glistened, and I think for sheer beauty
this day of travel surpassed any other of the whole summer.
Directly ahead was the " cold and restless mass " of Axel
Heiberg Glacier with its frozen falls and torrents and its
flatter, more placid stretches of ice; to the right was Mt.
Fridtjof Nansen, monarch of all the Queen Maud Range,
with his crown of shining ice; to the left were the steeper,
more slender slopes of Mt. Don Pedro Christopherson, and,
from our position as we turned to head up Axel Heiberg,
we could see this huge ice stream separated at its head by
a rock mass which we believed to be Amundsen's Mt. Wil-
liam Christopherson. It was uphill sledging all the way and

for the dogs just another day of heavy work, but for us who could coöperate, as it were, with what we saw all about us it was a day memorable for its beauty.

We stopped at Ipswich Beacon where I made some astronomical observations while Mike busied himself with his triangulation, and we then headed westward up the slopes of the ridge that we had to cross to reach Strom Camp. There was still a heavy blanket of soft snow all along the foot of the mountains, so that it was hard work for both the men and the dogs to make their way through it, and though it was but 8 miles farther to Strom Camp when we stopped for the day, we realized that it would have been needless cruelty to our dogs to have carried on for any such distance as that.

It seemed as if nature was out-doing herself to make our world colorful and Christmas-like as we stopped to make our camp on this morning of the 25th. Too often when the sun is bright it is only the snow far away that takes on color, that around one's feet and before his eyes as he trudges along is a dull chalky white. But strangely enough it was not so this morning. It was probably the loose blanket of snow that still covered everything that enabled the sun to turn it into myriad changing colors as we pushed our way through it. But even the most prosaic of us noticed the iridescence of the snow and commented upon our Christmas coloring.

We made camp at the foot of the eastern side of the mountain which we had believed to be Mt. Betty. With the additional knowledge from our eastern trip behind us, there seemed no other mountain that could fit Amundsen's designation and yet we could not be sure for we had failed to find the cairn which he had built on his Mt. Betty.

Our failure to definitely locate this mountain was the one great regret of our summer. Without knowing just which mountain Amundsen called by this name we could not be absolutely sure of the rest.

While I was preparing the evening hoosh Freddy was erecting the bamboo masts for his radio antennae, for I especially wanted him to get a " time tick." This camp was sort of a key position for our surveys and I wanted to locate it accurately. Had the radio served no other purpose than this of enabling us to keep accurate time it would have justified the extra trouble it necessitated to carry it along. The difficulty of keeping accurate time was probably the most prolific source of incorrectly charted positions by the earlier explorers. Only once in the course of the whole summer was Freddy unable to hear the time signals sent out from Arlington near Washington, D. C., and that with a small receiving set that he could easily carry under one arm.

Because one of the most irritating habits one can have on such a trek as this is that of trying to make conversation when no occasion for it exists, and because most subjects of conversation had long since grown rather threadbare, our meals were apt to be quiet. But on this 25th day of December we found some solace in discussing the Christmas dinner we had eaten on the 9th of November at depot number 2.

Sometimes as we sat about inside the cook tent waiting for the pot to boil, Mike would become so absorbed with his thoughts that he would start to sing. He knew one line of song that began, " Sweet violets, sweeter than all the world to me," and that was all. The summer was nearly gone before we discovered that Mike knew any other song, or perhaps any other words to this song for he sang all his songs to what sounded to me like the same tune. He once explained to me that such a system simplified things a great deal.

Freddy Crockett used to sing too, but almost without exception his need for expression found an outlet when he was putting up his radio. Of course, the song may have been a blind to keep his thoughts from finding more color- ful expression as he went about untangling his antennae, though I don't think so for Freddy was irrepressibly light- hearted. He always specialized on the Overture to Tann- hauser, making up the words as the themes progressed. As near as I could make out most of the words were, " Do, dee, dee, dum dum do dee dee ee." O'Brien was forever resing- ing a single line of a religious duet which went, " Since first thy soul was knit to mine." Eddie and Norman, rarely, if ever, even attempted to sing and as for myself my craving for expression in song always came out in my attempts to master the first two lines of, " The Lord is My Light." Cir- cumstances always somehow seemed to prevent me from getting much beyond those first lines.

When we roused ourselves at 7 o'clock that evening, which was, of course, our morning, we decided to make one last attempt to find the Amundsen cairn before we returned to Strom Camp. We had searched the whole top of the mountain without finding it and knew that it could not be there, but there was a shoulder of rock projecting northward into the snow about a thousand feet below the real top of the mountain. We had not previously examined this for it did not seem conceivable that Amundsen would have referred to this little ridge as " Mt. Betty." As we looked toward this ridge from our camp we could see a small piece or projection of rock that stood quite above its surroundings, but when we studied it through my field glasses it seemed to be just a single great piece of rock that had perhaps rolled down there from the mountain top or had been left stranded by glacial ice. We were so skeptical about this being the long-sought-for cairn that we did not think it wise to drive the dog teams the extra distance necessary to investigate it. Accordingly, we arranged that Mike and I would ski over to it, and if it were really the Amundsen cairn we would signal back to the rest with two trail flags which we took for this possible use.

It was a downhill slide so it took us but a few minutes to cover the three quarters of a mile that lay between our camp and the ridge of rock. The nearer we came to this curious projection of rock the more hopeful we became, yet we were almost upon it, before we realized that it was really built up of a number of smaller pieces of rock. Such a pile could only have been put together by man and the only men who had ever been within hundreds of miles of here were Amundsen and his polar party. We knew that it must be the work of their hands. I turned and waved my flags to those back in our camp who were watching us with their binoculars, and then Mike and I sat down to wait for them to come up with us.

Even the dogs seemed to sense the excitement in the air, for never had they covered three quarters of a mile in so short a time as they did these. It was almost with reverent hands that we took a few rocks from the side of the cairn so that we could see what was in it without in any way disturbing the shape or structure. We pulled out a five gallon tin can of kerosene or " paraffin " which, though it had been there for 18 years, was still quite intact and but little rusted, a waterproof package containing twenty small boxes of safety matches and a tin can with a tight lid on its top.

It was the climax, the high spot of the summer for all of us, when I pried off the lid of this tiny can and took out of it two little pieces of paper. One was just a piece rudely torn from a book and contained the names and addresses of Wisting and Johanssen who had helped Amundsen build the cairn, and the other was a page carefully torn from the notebook of Amundsen himself. We did not need to be able to read Norwegian to make out the fact that he had on this paper told of his successful achievement of the South Pole. I do not think anyone could have appreciated more fully than did the six of us all that lay behind that bit of paper and its simple account. We, too, had sledged over much of the same ice and snow that Amundsen and his party had crossed and we knew in a small measure, at least, what a wealth of experience and preparation and finally of physical prowess had made possible the modest message on this little piece of paper that we were holding in our hands. I think we shall none of us forget the glamour of that moment. When we arrived back in Little America Bernt Balchen translated the note for us:

6th — 7th of January, 1912

Reached and determined the Pole on the 14th to the 16th of December, 1911. Discovered the connection of Victoria Land and King Edward VII Land at 86 degrees south latitude and their continuation as a great mountain range towards the southeast. Have observed this range extending as far as 88 degrees south. Under the conditions of visibility that we had, it appeared to continue on farther in the same direction across the Antarctic Continent.

Passed this place on the return with provisions for 60 days, 2 sledges, 11 dogs. Everybody well.

Roald Amundsen

" Gee," said Freddy as he viewed the contents of the cairn, " he didn't leave any grub! " This might have been a jarring note from anyone but Freddy, who had the reputation of having the healthiest appetite of any man on the expedition — a rather unjust reputation I learned on the sledge journey for both Norman Vaughan and Mike Thorne ate more than he did.

We replaced the five gallon can of kerosene in the cairn but decided to bring back with us the matches and the note. Accordingly, I wrote a brief account of the geological sledge party on a page of my notebook and further stated that we were taking the matches and the note that Amundsen had originally left in the can. Then we replaced the rocks and left the cairn looking just as it had when Amundsen and his men had built it 18 years before. Each man was allowed to take some little bits of rock from it but not enough to disturb it in any way.

We were amazed, when we arrived at Strom Camp, to note the change that had taken place in our snow built depot. It seemed to have shrunk to half its original size. The great blocks of snow which we had carefully placed all around our supplies were honeycombed with holes, and icicles several inches in length were hanging from many of them. We were relieved to find that none of our supplies had been uncovered by this shrinkage of their snow covering, for in such a case the direct heat of the sun which is very great even here, would doubtless have turned our pemmican rancid. But we were a little worried about the contents of the depots we had established on our way to the mountains, for we had not covered the supplies we had left in them with such heavy blocks of snow as we had placed over everything here in Strom Camp. However, we did not expect that there would be as much " ablation " of the snow out on the shelf ice as there had been along the foot of the mountains. There were two reasons to expect more snow to disappear near the mountains — first from the direct heat absorbed by the steeper slopes of both the bare rock surfaces and the ice and snow surfaces, secondly from the effect of the chinook or foehn-like winds that blow down through the glacier troughs from the plateau. Whenever a wind is drawn down a considerable slope it is warmed — " adiabatically," the meteorologist calls it — which means that its capacity to hold water vapor is proportionately increased. Such dry winds may greatly deplete the snow, either through causing it to melt or by absorbing it directly by evaporation. Such winds are developed in places along the eastern slopes of the Rocky Mountains where they are called " snow eaters."

I was extremely anxious to make another journey up the flanks of Mt. Nansen to examine further the coal bearing rocks which I had prospected all too hastily in my eagerness to get started toward the east, but the dogs were tired and worn when we arrived in Strom Camp on the morning of the 26th day and my dog driving companions pointed out that it would be very unwise to drive them up the steep slopes of the glacier in their present weakened condition. Many would probably not have been able to do it, and we really could not afford to lose a single dog for we still had nearly 500 miles to go to get back to little America. In the end we decided to give the dogs a few days' rest, while we carefully overhauled our gear and took stock of our supplies, so that we might reduce our loads to a minimum weight before we started the long journey northward. This was most necessary for I had collected a considerable weight of rocks during the summer, which I purposed to bring back, and furthermore, we had to start with our dog power greatly reduced.

When we said good-bye to the supporting party on our way south, we had 46 dogs and now we had but 21 left. It had not been easy for us to face the fact that if we were to accomplish the things we had set out to do, it would be necessary to carry out fully the plans for the disposal of the dogs that we had made back in Little America before we started. This grim necessity which required us to kill so many of our dogs was the one thing that deprived our sledge journey of much of its romance. One would have to be more devoid of feeling than any of us were to have contemplated with equanimity the killing of these dogs of ours whom we had found to be possessed of so much personality and intelligence and with whom we had become such good friends. But not to do it meant the collapse of all our carefully worked out plans. We had to shut our eyes to sentiment or write the word failure as the end of all our efforts and careful planning. After all, I suppose if one deletes the matter of sentiment, there is little difference between the sacrifice of dogs for such necessity as faced us and the sacrifice of such animals as sheep and cattle for food, as happens as a complement to our daily living needs in our most civilized conditions. And the greatest cruelty to the dogs would have been to drive them on beyond the limits of their healthy endurance, for we disposed of the dogs that showed signs of weakening first.

Though we could not know it at the time, it was just

as well that we bade good-bye to our dogs out on the trail, for, as the final pages of our Antarctic days were written, they would in any case have had to be killed before we embarked for New Zealand. With the ice conditions so bad that only one of our two expedition ships was able to come through to the Bay of Whales to take us out, there would have been no room aboard for the dogs that we had been obliged to sacrifice. Yet in spite of all this, even now it makes me shudder when I think of these grand creatures pulling for us until in some cases they could do no more, only to be relieved by death, and their carcasses fed to their living companions that they might carry on and complete our journey for us.

It had been my thought that as we approached the sordid necessity of despatching our dogs' lives that it was a task of such an unpleasant nature that everyone should have to take part in it, with the provision, of course, that no one should have to kill his own dogs. But Norman insisted that the dogs were his responsibility and that this was part of his task. I will admit my own moral cowardice in too willingly giving in to him on this point. But the quiet way in which Norman carried out his work in this, and in all other respects, was one of the most satisfying things about the whole trip.

It was a source of wonder to all of us to see the way in which our young dogs stood the hard work. They had been little more than eight months old when we left Little America with them and one has no right to expect such heavy work from a dog as we exacted unless he is at least a year and a half old. We left Little America with five brothers of this very youthful age: they were Bob, Sky, Cocoa, Kit Carson, and Al Smith, and Kit Carson was the

only one who did not come back. I was glad to see Al
Smith distinguish himself for he was my own special dog
and a great dog he was in every way. I never saw a husky
who more sincerely wished peace; only when he was hard
pressed would he fight, he always tried to avoid trouble.
He was a bit of a diplomat, too, for he seemed to make a
point of keeping on good terms with his masters. Norman
drove him most of the time and whether in or out of harness he was always inviting Norman's attention to himself, quite apparently trying to ingratiate himself in his
driver's favor. He appeared to be successful in what he
started out to do, for even though he was altogether too
young to have any right to expect to be promoted to leadership, Norman decided one day to give him a trial. Al
knew what was expected of him and with all the assurance of a veteran he led off with the team behind him.

Al never shirked his duties and he bitterly resented seeing other dogs do so. I have seen him bark and snap at the
dog ahead of him trying to make him lean into the harness
and pull. In the early part of our homeward trek, when
Al was leading his team, he learned that the flags marked
the trail we were following. Occasionally we were able to
shorten our back trail by cutting across, but Al would have
none of this. He knew the flags were to be followed and
could only be dissuaded from doing so by being led away.

Leadership is an interesting thing among the dogs. Some
of the ablest dogs we had just could not be trained to lead.
Placed at the head of the team they had no notion of what
they were to do. As in men so it was in dogs, leadership
appeared to be a quality which was largely inherent. My
dog Al Smith had it! But of all our dogs, Freddy Crockett's
leader, Quimbo, was most conscious of the responsibilities

of his position, and was most jealous of any encroachments upon his prerogatives as the boss of his team. One day two dogs just behind him were snarling and showing their teeth at each other preliminary to a fight, but Quimbo did not wait for it, he took command of the situation and bit each dog rather savagely until they stopped their quarrelling. On another occasion the two wheel dogs, that is the pair of dogs next to the sledge, tangled in a fight, whereupon Freddy began to wield his whip in an attempt to separate them. When Quimbo turned around and sensed what was going on, without any hesitation at all he ran back and bit Freddy in the leg, for not even could Freddy, with whom he was on the friendliest terms and who had driven him for three years, interfere with his team!

Dinny, who had led Norman's team out from Little America, became a forlorn figure when he was removed from leadership to make way for my dog, Al Smith. His tail trailed between his legs and his ears lay back against his head, nor did he strain himself to do any work when his driver was not watching him. It was most amusing to see how promptly his traces would slacken when Norman slid up ahead on his skis where Dinny knew he could not see him. Then one day as we neared Little America on our return Norman decided to give Dinny back his old job again. What an instantaneous change took place in his attitude; ears at attention and tail curled over his back he was ready for work! But poor Al Smith could not understand why he had been brought back to his former lowly station and did not propose to tolerate it without protest. He could not bring himself to follow Dinny's lead and tried so hard to pull off to one side and induce the team to follow him rather than Dinny that he had to be disciplined.

Al Smith was something of an innovation in dogs' names. He happened to be born near a time when the ex-Governor of New York was broadcasting his greetings to the expedition and somebody suggested the name that he bore throughout his life. Depending on one's point of view he either lived up to his name or he lived it down, for there was no better dog in our whole pack than Al Smith. My dog driving companions had started in the early days of the expedition naming their dogs after other explorers and so we had Peary, Amundsen, Shackleton, Scott, Mawson, Bartlett, Fitz Green, Putnam and all the rest. After I tried to drive dogs myself I was inclined to dislike this method of naming them, for there are few if any dogs that do not have to be severely disciplined occasionally, and, of course, if one is given to such things he may forget and talk roughly to his dogs. It seemed a bit incongruous to me to beat up or talk harshly to a dog named Nansen or Scott. Then one day I found Eddie Goodale and Norman Vaughan trying to teach a dog to respond to the name of " Gould," and he was a very lowly creature, in fact one of the most unattractive dogs in the whole expedition. That settled my mind as to the propriety of naming dogs after people, for I could imagine the vicarious pleasures Eddie might have gotten from driving a dog named Gould and telling him what a no account creature he was. I protested about the name whereupon Eddie began calling the dog " Simon," insisting that it was after the famous Simple Simon!

When we assembled all of our equipment and supplies we found that we had a great deal more than our 21 tired dogs could possibly be expected to haul. We thereupon decided to leave the surplus inside a cairn over on Mt.

Betty near the one that Amundsen had built. We loaded all of our excess gear into our remaining Strom-Balchen sledge and hauled it over to Mt. Betty on the 29th where we heaped it up into a neat pile and then built a huge cairn of rocks around it. I placed a tin can inside this cairn with the supplies, containing a brief account of the trek of the geological sledge party and the account of our finding the Amundsen cairn which was but a few feet away. In the face of the necessity of cutting weights down to the very minimum before our homeward start, I even left one of my two rock hammers on the outside of this cairn. Finally we placed one of our trail flags on top of it, and then with more regrets than about anything else we had to abandon, we turned our last Strom-Balchen sledge up against the side of the cairn and turned our faces back toward Strom Camp. The return journey from Marie Byrd Land had cracked the runners of this fine sledge so badly that we did not dare take the risk of attempting to haul supplies back toward Little America upon it.

We had little regret as we looked forward to the journey back to Little America. We had been abundantly rewarded for the hard work we had been called upon to do.

We had climbed the slopes of Mt. Nansen and found the Beacon Sandstone with its seams of coaly material.

We had determined that the Queen Maud Mountains were a continuation of the extensive fault block mountains that mark the western boundary of the Ross Sea — that they were a part of the most extensive mountain system of this kind to be found anywhere in the world.

We had determined the correct direction of the course or trend of the Queen Maud Mountains, thus changing the previous geographical notions about this sector of the

SHACKLETON (ABOVE) AND HIS SON AL SMITH

Above: Fitz Green   Scott
Below: Dinny   Oolie

Antarctic. (Compare the map opposite page 70 based upon Amundsen's chart with that opposite page 124 to note the difference.)

We had added the final proof as to the non-existence of Carmen Land, thus removing a great supposed highland from the map.

Our sledge journey eastward to Marie Byrd Land had pushed the known limits of the Ross Shelf Ice more than a hundred miles farther east than it had been known to exist before.

Throughout all our journeyings about the mountains Mike Thorne had been busy with his surveying and had brought back a chart of some 200 miles of the Queen Maud Mountains; dozens of hitherto unknown ice capped peaks, many new glaciers some of which take their places among the very greatest known were added to the map. (See large map.)

Finally our crossing of the Ross Shelf Ice and our studies of the glaciers pushing down into it from the plateau behind the Queen Maud Mountains had added new information about its composition and its movements.

Of all Antarctic features the Ross Shelf Ice is most distinctive; it is unique in all the world. From the time of its discovery by Sir James Clark Ross in 1840, when he was searching for the South Magnetic Pole, to this very day it had been a source of wonder to all explorers who have been privileged to see it. If one is so fortunate as to approach it with a bright sun overhead he first sees the shelf ice as a northward facing cliff that looks like a dazzling white ribbon stretching away beyond the horizon both to the right and to the left. As he draws nearer the ribbon grows wider and finally he finds himself sailing along the foot of a snow-ice cliff that varies in height, from place to place, from 20 to 200 feet.

If the term " barrier " is to be used at all in connection with this vast expanse of shelf ice, it should be held to refer only to this great cliff which bounds it on the north and stretches for 500 miles across the southern navigable limits of the Ross Sea, and is in that sense a barrier to further voyaging. For the whole floating sheet of snow-ice the term " Ross Shelf Ice " is the most appropriate for it is the most truly descriptive.

One finds little change in the character of the shelf ice as he sails along it or sledges across it. It is ever a flat or gently rolling limitless plain of snow. By all tokens it should be monotonous, but it rarely seemed to affect us in that way for its charm lies not so much in its actual scenic beauty as in the feeling that it gives one. There is an atmosphere, an impression, an intangible something that is intriguing.

It is interesting to note that the " barrier " or the front of the Ross Shelf Ice, receded from twenty to thirty miles toward the south between the time of its discovery by Ross in 1840 and its first re-survey by Scott in 1902; but from the time of this first survey by Scott down to the present time only minor changes in its latitude have taken place. Yet we know that along much of its front it is being pushed northward at an appreciable rate. Alternate surveys made by Scott and Shackleton near its western limits show that there the shelf ice is advancing at the rate of at least 1000 feet per year, but curiously enough the front stays in approximately the same place. In other words just about as fast as the shelf ice is pushed forward it breaks off to float away as the tabular white " snowbergs " which are so characteristic of the seas around the Antarctic. We do not have accurate measurements of the rate of movement along any other portion of the shelf ice front, but major changes in outline have taken place from time to time all along the western portion without appreciably changing the latitude. Interestingly enough the eastern portion, or roughly that part from Discovery Inlet eastward to King Edward VII Land, does not seem to have been much disturbed. For instance, the Bay of Whales has been a distinct feature certainly since Scott's first charting of it in 1902 and does not seem to have changed its position in any essentials since that time.

One needs but look at the map to understand the source of the power that is causing this forward movement. On all sides where it has been mapped, that is to the west and the south, the Ross Shelf Ice is seen to be bounded by high block mountains, many of which are widely separated by great troughs occupied by vast glaciers bringing down their huge streams of ice from the plateau behind. Very rough measurements of the mouths of these valley or outlet glaciers that have been charted show that if all were taken together they would comprise a single stream of ice more than 150 miles wide! The only escape or outlet for the shelf ice is toward the north.

Since some of the greatest glaciers enter the shelf ice south of the Bay of Whales one might wonder why the ice front here is not more disturbed and moved northward, and why the most pronounced movements take place along the western side. Here again the map answers the question. First it will be noted that Beardmore, which is the mightiest of all the glaciers, directs its flow almost due north along the western side of the shelf ice. Secondly though

Amundsen, Thorne, Axel Heiberg, and Liv Glaciers flow
down from the plateau toward the north, this direction is
largely offset by the great overpowering volume of ice from
Leverett Glacier which almost parallels the mountain
front from the east. The net result of all these confluent
streams of ice is a general direction of ice flow toward the
northwest from the vicinity of Axel Heiberg Glacier in
such a way that the combined push of all these glaciers is
added to that from Beardmore.

There is an additional, and probably a more important,
reason why the Bay of Whales has so long escaped de-
struction. Even though the Ross Shelf Ice appears to be
afloat throughout most of its known extent there are places
where it is stranded on land, and it is due to just this fact
that the Bay of Whales is protected. Unquestionably the
great hill south of Little America, which we crossed on
our way to and from the Queen Maud Mountains, is an
ice covered island. Furthermore, the crevasses which we
crossed between latitudes 81 and 82 degrees south and
those discovered by Admiral Byrd farther west in longitude 170, indicate the presence of islands or at least reefs
that help to stem the northward flow of the ice.

There has been a good deal of speculation as to the
origin of the Ross Shelf Ice, and I believe most students
of the problem agree that there have been two important
sources for the materials of which it is composed. First
the glacial ice that flows down from the plateau, and, secondly land-locked or " ice-locked " masses of sea ice upon
which successive snows have accumulated. I think it is not
difficult to visualize the roles played by each of these
sources. Let one imagine a condition, as a start, with the
waters of the Ross Sea washing the lower slopes of the

fault block mountain boundary. With the accumulation of snow and ice on the plateau, the great valley or outlet glaciers would begin to form and flow down into the Ross Sea. The streams of glacial ice from these outlets would be rigid, and would thus extend out into the waters of the Ross Sea like ribs, or fingers, or better still, considering a number of them together, like the skeletal toes of a hen's foot, done on a gargantuan scale. Then let one imagine the sea between these ribs or toes to be frozen over and the hen's foot to become the web foot of a duck, then I think, we visualize the essential foundations of the great Ross Shelf Ice. Drifting snow would gradually build up the hollows between the ribs and the whole would come to have a fairly common level and as the snow became more compacted, a more uniform rigidity. From the observation made on our travels, it seemed to me that, quantitively, formation upon a sea ice base had been the more important source.

I have referred in a previous chapter to the fact that we found evidence that the ice cover on the plateau must at a former time have been much thicker than now, and previous students have found widespread evidence that in former times the continental ice cap in all of its ramifications must have been much more extensive than now. It is quite right to think of the present ice cap as a relic of a much greater ice mass, which existed here when other parts of the world were also in the grip of the so-called great Ice Age, when both northern Europe and northern North America as far south as the Ohio and Missouri Rivers were covered by huge sheets of ice which must have been similar in their essential aspects to the one that still covers most of Antarctica. At that time of maximum glaciation many mountains now exposed were smothered beneath the ice, and it is estimated that the Ross Shelf Ice was so thick that it rested on the bottom of the sea and extended some three hundred miles farther northward than now.

Soundings demonstrate that the present shelf ice is afloat along its entire front; definite currents flow in and out beneath the ice; and it is believed that its fairly uniform height and the fact that seasonal accumulations of snow do not greatly affect it are due to the fact that it is largely afloat throughout its extent, and that there is a rough balance between the rate of supply and depletion from above with the melting from below.

CHAPTER X

THE RETURN TO LITTLE AMERICA

" it was mine by right.
Doubtless a searching and impetuous soul
Might learn from its own motions that some task
Like this awaited it about the world;
Might seek somewhere in this blank life of ours
For fit delights to stay its longings vast;
And grappling Nature, so prevail on her
To fill the creature full she dared thus frame
Hungry for joy: "

BROWNING

IT was a small, and not too lively pack of dogs with which we had to begin the homeward journey to Little America. Though they had revived somewhat from their arduous journey to Marie Byrd Land and return, they were still worn from the hard summer, and we knew that we could not push them too hard. Our sledges were somewhat battle scarred too; even the largest of our Norwegian sledges which was still usable, had suffered a cracked runner.

Eddie and Norman thought it might help the dogs along with their loads if they put sails on their sledges, for we were sure from our experience with the winds on our way south, that as we headed northward, they would be on our backs or on our starboard quarter at least, most of the time. Ours was a picturesque train for Eddie had equipped his sledge with a single sail that made it resemble a badly rigged sloop, while Norman had held out for a square sail which made his sledge look not unlike a Chinese junk. Freddy had watched proceedings without comment, but with a superior sort of air, and made no attempt to equip his sledge for sailing. Under ordinary circumstances the sails would doubtless have been of considerable help, but the 20 days that were consumed in our journey back to Little America were singularly free from strong winds — as winds blow in the Antarctic. And many that we did have were from the wrong quarter.

The mountains about us had been obscured in clouds since the return from our eastern journey, and as if for a good omen, the sky partially cleared just as we were getting started. The sight to the south of us was just what we would all have most liked to preserve as our last intimate view of the mountains. No one can delve into the history of polar exploration at all without frequently coming across the name of Fridtjof Nansen. He was really the father of polar exploration in its modern scientific sense and contributed more to it than any man who has yet lived; for this reason as well as for the fact that it was the loftiest and most imposing mountain that we had seen, and had given us the key to the geology of the whole range, the great mass named for him had come to hold first place in the affections of all of us. With our dogs harnessed and hitched to the sledges, waiting for the command to go, we turned for a last look, and there behind us was grand old Nansen with his cap of shining ice glistening in the bright sun, and his dark shoulders of partly bare rock, still wrapped about in a ragged old shawl of clouds that the sun had not yet dispersed. It was a perfect end to our mountain summer.

To have retraced our steps through the crevasses below Liv Glacier that had made the last day of our journey to reach the mountains fraught with so much uncertainty would have been little short of madness. We had long since decided that it would be far wiser to abandon all thought of following the trail and strike out toward the north directly away from the mountains until we had cleared the crevassed zone, and then trust to the accuracy of our navigation to enable us to relocate our trail.

It was 1 o'clock on the morning of December 30th when we left Strom Camp. It was downhill travelling all the " afternoon " and by 5:30 we had covered 25 miles. We had crossed a few crevasses some of which were very large but not at all comparable to those farther west that we were trying to avoid.

After our customary sleep we were off again with the sledges still gliding along easily over the hard surface. We reasoned that we had passed beyond the crevassed zone by the middle of the morning and we therefore directed our course a little more to the westward so as to pick up our old trail as soon as possible. Our dead reckoning calculations indicated that we should cross the trail before the end of the day. Naturally as the afternoon passed we were all straining our eyes more and more anxiously — looking for flags or snow beacons. About 4 o'clock Freddy shouted that he could see a beacon almost dead ahead of us. None of the rest of us could see it at first, but we had not gone on much farther until it was plain to all of us. Freddy had the best eyes. We hit the trail within a half mile of where we had reckoned we would.

We camped that night (the 31st) at the snow beacon which had marked the place of our departure for our last day's 40 mile " dash " to the mountains. Here again we were amazed to note how greatly the beacon had diminished in size since we had built it little more than a month previously. Very evidently the warm winds that sweep down from the mountains, and had so greatly depleted the snow over our depot at Strom Camp, had had a pronounced effect way out here.

The New Year began with a dull overcast day and with a light breeze from the east, right on our beam. The breeze was a good thing, for the visibility was generally poor but the flags were blown out by it just right for us to see them to best advantage. In less than six hours travelling time we had arrived at depot number 7. Much melting and evaporation of the snow had occurred here. The outer blocks about the depot were honeycombed and had icicles several inches long hanging from them, but no harm had been done for none of our supplies had been exposed to the sun.

The farther northward we went, the more we appreciated the fact that we had marked the trail so well when we were southward bound. When the sun was bright its light was reflected from the snow beacons with a " blink " that we could see from 4 to 6 miles away — a much greater distance than we could ever see any of the flags, even those on top of the beacons. On the other hand when the sky was overcast we couldn't see the snow beacons at all; then the flags were indispensable and since our weather was more often cloudy than not, the flags were generally of much greater service than were the snow beacons. The combination of the two could scarcely be improved upon. Sometimes we travelled in fog so dense that a person driving beside the front team could not see the second team behind him. Of course we could not see the flags any distance under such conditions but it was most reassuring to come upon them at fairly regular intervals. They told us that we were keeping on the trail, though we were steering not by them at all but by the compass.

We arrived at depot number 6 shortly after noon on the 3rd, and stopped long enough to dig out our supplies and lash them onto our sledges. We found that there had been no appreciable melting or evaporation of the snow blocks which covered our supplies here. Evidently we had gotten beyond the zone affected by the warm dry winds that blow down the mountains from the plateau.

We were in such excellent physical condition from the hard work of the summer that we travelled along with great ease, especially as compared with the hard work that had accompanied our southward trek. But the dogs were showing the effects of the gruelling summer's work and we had to be careful for their sake, and, purely on their account, we decided to limit ourselves to 23 miles per day. Some days when the surface made sledging easy for them we made good this distance within six or seven hours, nevertheless we forced ourselves not to get impatient but stopped and made camp.

There were no rocks to examine, no mountains to climb, nothing that I could do in the way of physical labor when we were not travelling, and a ski journey of 23 miles was scarcely a day's work any more. These days came nearer to being monotonous than had any other part of the summer. Time *did* hang heavily on our hands. To me the continuous daylight was a large contributory factor to this near monotony. Throughout every day we had to wear colored snow glasses; our tents were made of white cloth with just a small patch of colored cloth over the top to cut the most intense glare of the sun, but still the light was bright within them. I used to long for the soothing velvety feel of the darkness on my eyes. I really believe that this unending light was far more tiresome to me than had been the long dark. There is much more variety in a polar night than there is in a polar day, and besides, one can create light when he tires of the darkness. But there was no way for us to induce even semi-darkness. We had to stand the light and when we had completed our whole day's work within eight to ten hours, I found it impossible to spend the rest of the time sleeping. There is a real relationship between darkness and the desire and need for sleep. No matter how hard we worked we never seemed to crave as much sleep as we would have under ordinary conditions of alternating periods of daylight and darkness.

I don't know just what I should have done with all my free time had it not been for the few books that we had brought along with us. Each man had been allowed one book and ordinarily I should have brought Browning with me, but I had been reading him off and on all winter and elected to bring a thin paper edition of Shakespeare, complete in one volume. I regaled myself with Hamlet and Macbeth and King Lear and Love's Labor Lost and The Passionate Pilgrim, trying to fall asleep. When the day's journey had been particularly easy we would have supper over and be finished with the work for the day, ofttimes as early as 6 o'clock. I would crawl into my bag and lie there and read until 12 o'clock or later before going to sleep.

But I ran out of Shakespeare. One doesn't realize how much reading he can cover when he has five to seven hours per day without any kind of interruption. It had never before occurred to me that one of the real advantages and benefits of an Antarctic Expedition would be the opportunity to read Shakespeare in his entirety. I have never appreciated all the tragedy of Lear quite so much as I did in this reading of it — out in the midst of the Ross Shelf Ice.

Mike Thorne had brought along W. H. Hudson's " Purple Land " and though I had read it but a few weeks previously, I read it again with the delight I always find in Hudson's exquisite prose. Eddie Goodale had brought a volume of English poetry which I devoured and in which I was glad to find one of my great favorites by Browning, " The Bishop Orders His Tomb." O'Brien had a big thick volume containing H. G. Wells short stories. I read this too, and it would have afforded me no end of satisfaction to have dropped this volume down the deepest crevasse I could find, but O'Brien objected strongly. He had borrowed the book from Russell Owen who wanted it returned.

On the 4th we encountered the worst sledging surface that we had found since leaving the mountains. It was typical pie crust snow; that is there was but a weak crust on the snow which was insufficient to bear either the weight of the dogs or that of the sledges. The dogs' feet broke through and they went waddling along almost up to their bellies. It was frightfully hard work for them just to trot along but it was made much harder, because the sledges, even with their wide wooden runners, would not stay on the weak crust but went crashing their way through rather than gliding easily over the top as they ordinarily did.

Just about noontime, which was our midnight, the clouds lifted behind us to reveal a thin clear streak all about our horizon and to give us our very last view of the Queen Maud Mountains. They were now just a narrow ribbon of ice capped peaks so far away that they seemed scarcely real.

The 5th was a raw overcast day with the surface worse than ever and the sledging correspondingly hard for the dogs. Sometimes it was very foggy with consequent poor visibility and an almost continuous cutting wind from the southeast, but we plodded along persistently, for we wanted to reach depot number 5 before we stopped. If we were in for a spell of bad weather we much preferred to have it come when we were at a depot, for we were not able to carry very large reserves between these caches without overloading the dogs. My bags of rocks had not gotten any lighter.

On the 6th the sun reappeared completely for the first time since we had left the mountains. Its direct rays seemed frightfully warm; we surprised even ourselves at the small amount of clothing that we needed to keep us warm as we skied along beside our sledges. Unprotected from its glare by the clouds, we found our sleeping bags too warm inside our tents that night.

It didn't seem as if sledging conditions could get any worse, but on the 8th we ran into the worst surface that we had yet struck. It brought back to us memories of the trouble we had had crossing this same stretch on our way south. We had found our hardest work here and on one day had made but 9 miles. With the lapse of nearly 2 months the surface had not gotten any better and the dogs found it next to impossible to waddle along and still pull the sledges through the soft snow. When we had covered 15 miles we stopped for the day, but even so we had stopped at depot number 4 at 2 o'clock and taken on fresh reserves of food and fuel.

Though our work had grown much harder during the past few days on account of the effort necessary to push our skis through the loose or lightly crusted snow, I still had the same nightly trouble about sleeping enough to fill up a large portion of my idle time. I find this entry in my diary at the end of the 8th:

" But even with my reading I didn't sleep until 12:30 and got up at 5:45 and have been active all day. I cannot persuade myself to sleep to-night, even though it is 11 o'clock. I have just finished reading Henry IV and have been stupidly playing solitaire with the cards jumbled about on top of my sleeping bag and still my eyes will not close. I did close them a little while ago and recited all the poetry I knew, and then started on the psalms but somehow ran out of the latter rather quickly, and here I am writing this drivel just because I can't sleep — anyhow the sun is bright and the sky is clear toward the north so we may have good weather for the next few days to take us across the crevasses."

And once one fell asleep he was not always sure of peaceful slumbers. Many of my nights seemed to be taken up with food dreams. Our rations had been abundant and quite as varied as any party had ever had under similar circumstances. I never heard anyone complain of not having enough to eat, but I had never liked oatmeal since I had to eat it as a child, and, excellent food though it is, pem-

mican was never tasteful to my palate. I have found myself
sitting at a table fairly sagging with the things I was long-
ing for and just as I would reach for a piece of fried
chicken, something always happened. Usually it seemed to
be a sort of paralysis that prevented me from touching the
plate of chicken. I remember being aroused once from a
half awake condition, with the profound feeling that if
I could just have (of all things) all the canned salmon I
wanted I would ask nothing more in this life. Curiously
enough though they had never been my most favored food,
more often than not I dreamed of strawberries and cream.
Time after time I would fill a big spoon with the red
berries swimming in rich yellow cream, but invariably
through one cause or another I never got a bite. Often I
awoke just as the spoon reached my mouth.

What to do with one's mind during the day was often
somewhat of a problem too. I had reviewed the geological
and geographical results of the past weeks from all possible
angles until the very thought of a rock was something to
be shied away from. There was nothing about one to afford
variety or to stimulate one's thinking or direct it into
new channels. A few words of a poem or a snatch of a song
would start running through my mind and try as I would
I could not get rid of it. The more incongruous they
were the more tenaciously did they stick. One day I had
grown fairly tired when I remembered that ever inspiring
promise of Isaiah that:

" They that wait upon the Lord shall renew their
strength — they shall mount up with wings as eagles, they
shall run and not be weary; they shall walk and not faint."
And ridiculous as it sounds, my mind became obsessed
with the paradoxical complaint that Isaiah had neglected

THE DOGS DIDN'T MIND THE BLIZZARDS

COCOA AND AL SMITH TAKE A REST

MIKE THORNE   NORMAN VAUGHAN

FREDDY CROCKETT   EDDIE GOODALE
HOW THEY LOOKED AT THE END OF THE TREK

to give any comfort to those who travelled on skis! I could think of nothing else the whole day!

Toward the end of the afternoon of the 8th we could see parts of the broken surface of the crevassed area looming up ahead of us. It was the last hazard that separated us from the completion of our task, and of course we were more than fervently hoping that all of the clouds would disappear before we had to attempt to cross this area. We knew that it should not be tried except with excellent visibility.

The surface was so soft when we started out on the 9th that it was necessary to break some sort of trail for the dogs. I skied out in front of the teams behind Mike, making separate tracks so that between us we made sort of a roadway for the dogs. In the afternoon I was sliding along behind Mike with my mind in a state of " thoughtful vacuum," paying little attention to things about me. Now and again I could hear a driver calling to his dogs and I thought all of the teams were right behind me. At 3 o'clock Mike and I stopped for a rest and turned around to see how things were going with the dogs and we could not see a single team. A thick opaque wall of fog hid everything to the south of us. We had gone too fast for we had to wait 40 minutes for the rest of the party to come up with us. We travelled a little more slowly then and kept closer together.

When we were ready to break camp on the 10th we found the fog had gotten thicker than ever. We could see but a few feet ahead of us and were continually getting off the trail. We didn't want the dogs to have to do a lot of extra work on account of our meanderings, so we took one of the small trailer sledges and mounted the boat compass upon it. Mike hauled this along behind him, and I skied along beside it keeping a check on the course. Mike was able to keep the compass on a much more even keel than was possible with a dog drawn sledge. We kept to the trail quite well this way, but if we went along without seeing any flags for a considerable length of time, we stopped the teams and made little journeys off to the right and to the left until we had relocated the trail. We did not lose a great deal of time this way for we never allowed ourselves to get very far off the main track.

The fog remained thick throughout the day and when we thought we were nearing the margin of the crevassed zone, we stopped and made camp. We had no wish to get into the crevasses without seeing our way — much less did we have any intention of attempting to cross them until the visibility improved.

As we sat around our supper that night we might easily have imagined ourselves to be in the midst of a bombardment. For as the ice snapped and cracked all around and under us from the strains that were upon it, the resulting noises sounded like sharp cracks of rifles, or if from some depth, like the muffled roars of light field pieces some distance away. Now and then the ice would crack right under our tent and give us a little jar. We were disturbed about these things at first, but shortly got used to them for we felt sure that if we had not camped on the roof of a crevasse the likelihood of a fresh one opening up beneath us, large enough to let us fall in, was very remote. We had watched the ice break to form new crevasses and had never seen a newly made crack more than a very few inches wide. It appears that when the ice makes its initial break from being under strain, cracks of this order of size are formed and continued strains cause them to grow until, in some cases, they get as large as were some that we had crossed in front of Liv Glacier. We saw no crevasses of great width that had any signs at all of being freshly formed. So we went to sleep without much fear of being engulfed in a new born crevasse.

After I had gotten into my sleeping bag I pulled out my stop watch to time the frequency of the cracks that were going on about us. I counted them for 20 minutes and found that they averaged one per second. I fell asleep counting them, and woke about three hours later. I listened in vain for our fusillade. There was never a sound, yet when we started moving about again the next morning, our bombardment began all over again. It appeared that even though the ice was as much as 600 to 700 feet thick, it was yet under such a delicately balanced strain that the mere weight of our little party upon it disturbed it enough to start it breaking. I took special notice of this phenomenon during our stay among the crevasses and am convinced that the cracking just described was not primarily a function of temperature changes or any other meteorological conditions.

We had been greeted by this same sort of noisy barrage, though on a smaller scale, when we were camped 70 miles north of the mountains on our way home. We were amazed by this first bombardment for the surface was smooth all about us and we knew of no crevasses within 50 miles of us. Perhaps this location represents roughly the shearing zone between the relatively stagnant shelf ice to the north and the more active portion adjacent to the mountains on the south.

In the course of our work about the mountains we had

often been camped on and near active glaciers, but nowhere else than in these two places were we so noisily
saluted.

The 11th was too foggy to move ahead, but it was so
hard to sit still and our food supply was getting so short,
that finally Freddy, Mike, and I put on our skis and set out
to explore the trail ahead of us. The flags had been set
close together throughout the crevassed area and we were
able to follow them fairly well, so we assumed that when
the fog lifted, we should be able to follow the old route
with relatively little difficulty.

That night when the rest were in bed, I became so restless that I found my sleeping bag intolerable. I knew that
we had to move on toward our next depot within the next
two or three days or kill some dogs for food. I was unduly
impatient and did quite the most foolish thing I have ever
done. Throughout the summer I had never let any of the
men with me go off alone, and here I found myself preparing to do something that I would not have permitted any
two of them to do. I was putting on my skis to see if I could
not follow the trail along a little farther than we had gone
this morning, with the hope that I might find it feasible to
attempt to go through with our teams without waiting
longer for good weather.

I slid out beyond the part that Mike, Freddy, and I had
explored and all went well for a while, for I could follow
the closely spaced flags. I was headed straight for one when
suddenly the snow gave way beneath me. I threw myself forward as I felt the surface sink and my skis caught against the
walls of the crevasse so I did not get a severe fall. I dug holes
into the walls and shortly had myself on top. I turned and
looked down into the blue-black depths from which my

long skis had saved me, got up and very meekly retraced my steps to our camp. I had demonstrated at almost too great expense, that we should not be able to follow back along our former trail, at least for parts of the way. New cracks had opened up or the roofs of old ones had fallen in across the path that had seemed perfectly solid when we had crossed it some two months previously. I quietly crawled into my bag intending never to say a word about my folly to my companions.

Toward morning I awoke to find that the air had cleared of its fog and that the sky was thinly covered with alto-cumulus clouds with prospects of a clearer day ahead. I immediately called my companions for we could not afford to waste any time.

For the first time since we had made camp in this spot, we were able to get some notion of our surroundings. We discovered that we had really not stopped just south of the crevassed area as we thought. In fact we had pitched our camp between two great crevasses from three to ten feet wide, which were open in places and but thinly roofed over in others. Our skis had enabled us to cross these in safety without even suspecting their presence, but had we stopped to make our camp ten feet farther on or ten feet sooner, and then taken off our skis to stake out the dogs and put up the tents, there is little doubt but that some of us would have fallen into one of these partially blind chasms. We decided to sound these crevasses but the longest line we had was only 250 feet in length and that did not reach bottom, so we only know that they were deeper than that.

Mike, O'Brien, Freddy, and I put on our skis and started out to prospect a new way, for it was light enough so we dared travel.

"Who could have been skiing way out here?" said one of the three as he saw my tracks. They were all immediately suspicious so I could only hold my tongue and try to divert their attention to something else. It was no use.

"Simon would never have let one of us get off alone like this," volunteered Mike.

On we went until my ski tracks disappeared into the crevasse.

"And look," said O'Brien, "what a stupid ass he was to go and jump right into that crevasse. I wonder who it could have been."

Of course all three knew whose tracks these were and it was long before I was allowed to forget this episode.

We found an easy way past the crevasses into which I had stumbled, and hastened back to bring on the teams. We were on our way at 4:30 and had easily crossed a large part of the most broken up areas when suddenly in the very midst of a spider web of crevasses the sky and all about us disappeared into an opaque white gloom. We could see nothing. We dared hardly take a step and had to crowd ourselves somewhat to find space large enough to set up our tents and stake out the dogs. There were cracks on every side of us and we had crossed the roof of one to reach the place where we were camped. There was nothing to do but wait for clearer weather even though we had a scant twenty-four hours' food for the dogs.

We slept through the night and awoke on the morning of the 13th to find the world a little less opaque, but still dangerous weather for travelling. But we had to start this day or kill some dogs. We wanted to avoid this if at all possible so Mike, Norman, and I roped ourselves together and set forth to see if we could not find an easier way out of the crevasses than that by which we had crossed when we were southward bound. In spite of the poor visibility this turned out to be much simpler than we had dreamed it could be. We found that by going directly north from our camp we would come out of the crevasses almost immediately.

No time in the course of the summer had we camped in the midst of such a maze of crevasses as we had stopped in here. Naturally we expected another bombardment such as we had had at our last camp. I took out my stop watch after I had gotten into my sleeping bag to time the sounds here to see how they compared in frequency with those of our previous camp. I fell asleep with my watch in my hand without having heard a single sound. I then realized more fully than before that the active forces causing the ice movement were directed from a southerly direction. Only on that side had we found sharp new cracks whereas when we approached from the north we found only old crevasses filled with ice and snow and obviously long since inactive.

Naturally the question arose among us as to whether it was wiser to take the new route we had found and take the chance of picking up our regular trail before we came to depot number 3, or to wait a few hours in the hopes that better visibility would enable us to follow the flags. We did not hesitate much about abandoning the old trail, for marked though it was, it was much more hazardous than the new way we had found. We sledged northward over the route prospected by Norman, Mike, and me, until we thought we were beyond the crevassed zone and then swung toward the west, hoping to pick up our trail. Our dead reckoning was again good enough for we found our trail within a mile of where we had expected to.

We arrived at our depot number 3 at noon of the 14th.

We stopped for lunch and took on a welcome supply of food and fuel and were on our way again. For the first time in nearly a week the sun shone for a little while this day.

On the morning of the 15th I was up at 6 P.M. as usual and by 8:30 we had started the day's trek intending to do our customary 23 miles. But it was a bitter day; overcast and foggy with the bad visibility that went with such combination and with a nasty north to northwest wind that threw snow into our faces and stung our eyes. We would have stopped when we had covered 18 miles but we could not see a flag ahead of us, and decided that we had best be sure we were on the trail before stopping for the day. We drove on for four miles, making occasional searches on either side, before we found a flag. It appeared that there must have been a narrow zone through here which had been swept by inordinately high winds for though we had found individual flags blown down here and there we had never come across another such barren stretch in the whole trip.

With the end of our journey almost in sight, as it were, we were beginning to anticipate more and more eagerly not only a change in diet but the luxury of getting clean again. We had not been able to carry fuel enough to enable us to have water for toilet purposes. Our fuel rations were based solely on the needs of our cooking; we were unable to wash any of our clothing and could only attempt to wash our persons with snow. This was far from satisfactory and all of us showed evidences of the " Antarctic Disease " in various stages of development. Nobody attempted to shave and only Mike and O'Brien had clipped their beards. Two of Shackleton's men, Marston and Murry, long ago suggested a method for having some clean clothing which we copied. This method only works if one has two of any article of clothing with which to start. For instance one can always have a clean shirt in this way; put shirt number 1 on and wear it until it gets so dirty that one can't stand it; take it off and put on shirt number 2 and wear this one until it is twice as dirty as shirt number 1 which will now seem clean by comparison! Then change back to shirt number 1 and so on as long as the shirts last!

There was some commotion among us when on the morning of the 16th we received the following radiogram from Little America:

Larry:

There is a chance that the New York and Bolling may not get through ice this year only two of the seven whaling factories have gotten through ice stop they may go north of ice pack soon as there are very few whales south of the pack stop if we don't go with them we may not get back this year therefore I have asked them if they would send two chasers down here to take us back in case they go north before the Bolling or New York gets through pack stop Freddy had better give us radio schedule every day so we can keep you posted on developments.

Byrd

Then followed as unpleasant a day as we had had since leaving the mountains. A thin layer of hoar frost had settled on the snow while we slept and as was always true when this happened, the surface over which we had to travel was more like sand than snow. A heavy penetrating fog that came and went in great waves throughout the day made it one of the meanest days for sledging and skiing that we had ever had, for even though the temperature was above zero, it was the kind of wet cold that chilled one through. We had all worked hard to cover our customary 23 miles. With the uncertainty of conditions attendant on our getting away from Little America we should have gone farther but it would have been hard on the dogs.

And then as Freddy sat in his tent after supper clicking away with his radio came this message:

Larry — Rush:
I have requested the Nielson Alonzo Whaling Factory to call here for the expedition it will take them about two days to get here if they agree to come please hustle all you can as it is difficult to hold the factory up we hear from them this morning so you had better give us a schedule tomorrow morning so that we can give you the dope cheerio.

Byrd

We were still 104 miles from Little America and there was much discussion as to whether the dogs could cover such a distance within two days. There would have been little question about it had they been fresh. I believe Eddie was the most disturbed of us all. He wanted to get home and with right good reason. Except for a similar reason, nothing could have pleased me more than to have had the opportunity of spending another Antarctic night, with the following summer for a sledge journey eastward from Little America.

On the morning schedule came the following message:

Larry:
Got word from whalers this morning they will be unable to come for us so you can take things easy the rest of the way.

Byrd

We were all relieved by this message for we preferred the further uncertainty of getting away from Little

America to the necessity of driving our tired and heavily loaded dogs so many miles in two days. It could have been done: these dogs of ours could do almost anything, but we had punished them enough. It had always seemed to me that the great distances Peary had been obliged to cover during the last few days before he reached the North Pole were almost impossible. I know now that they were not and that no one who has not lived and worked with dogs can by any manner of means appreciate the extent of their endurance.

We knew that we should pass the snowmobile on the 17th. We had long since run out of cigarettes and tobacco and all manner of substitutes had been tried with but little success. Eddie Goodale once attempted to smoke a pipeful of unused senna grass. The rest of the party rose up as one man to protest against a repetition of the experiment. O'Brien seemed to miss these things more than anyone else, and, on the mere hope that there might have been a package of cigarettes or some tobacco left at the snowmobile, was all impatience to get there. He did not wait for the rest of us to finish our lunch before he was off on his skis.

When we arrived at the snowmobile about 2 o'clock there sat O'Brien in the seat puffing away at a much discolored and poorly repaired cigarette of a brand that is probably more scorned by men than any other kind. He had found half a package of these cigarettes and now passed them around to the rest of us with a very grand manner.

We crossed the big hill on the north slopes of which our depot number 1 was located and stopped only long enough to take on a few supplies. It was easy going for the dogs so we travelled 35 miles before stopping to make our last camp on the morning of the 18th.

We had not gone far on our way on the 19th when we came upon fresh ski tracks. We thought it strange that anybody should have been skiing 25 miles south of Little America so recently. Shortly we saw a man on skis headed toward us. We were almost upon him before we recognized Dr. Coman. It was pleasant to have Dana be the first to welcome us back. He with Quinn Blackburn and Alexander were camped at the head of the Bay of Whales, where they were doing some surveying, and that was how they happened to be the first to greet us. Van der Vere, who never missed an opportunity to get a picture, was out here at this surveying camp to get some movies before we had a chance to clean up at Little America.

Not until we had cleared the low hills to the south of Little America and saw the radio towers in the distance ahead did we fully realize that our long trek was over. In the course of all our journeyings with side trips we had covered 1525 miles. We didn't like to think it was over and when we turned for a last look back over the trail we had made, and realized that even then the wind was filling it with snow and soon the old shelf ice would be as unbroken as before, it made me somewhat sad. But my heart was filled with a great joy too, for I knew that even though the physical exaltation of a great adventure was gone, I would yet always have it, and would always be able to

"recall that sweep of savage splendor,
   That land that measures each man at his worth,
   And feel again in memory, half fierce, half tender
   The brotherhood of men who knew the south."

Chapter XI

WHY?

Poor vaunt of life indeed,
Were man but formed to feed
On joy, to solely seek and find and feast
Such feasting ended, then
As sure an end to men:

BROWNING

The history of the human race is a continual struggle from darkness toward light. It is therefore to no purpose to discuss the use of knowledge; man wants to know and when he ceases to do so, he is no longer man.

NANSEN

WHY? What for? What is the practical use of it all? These are the commonest questions that have been asked me about polar exploration and about the Byrd Antarctic Expedition in particular. It has been an interesting, if somewhat dismal, realization to find that people in general are more concerned with *why* we went to the Antarctic than they are with *what we brought back!*

I suppose that from a money mad people which hesitates from habit to invest in anything that holds no promise of immediate dividends, such a reaction is not to be wondered at. But it is none the less depressing. To that oft recurring question — What for? — I once answered, in a moment of irritation, with the counter question: " What good is any kind of learning, what use is knowledge anyhow? " And I believe it is generally true, that to the sort of person for whom the idea of the love of knowledge for its own sake is something of a mystery, there is not much use to attempt to answer that question.

But there are many who will realize and understand that whether the knowledge to be gained from further Antarctic exploration and research is of any immediate practical use or not, is in no sense fundamental. For in a large sense, all knowledge, no matter how abstract, is useful. If one goes back to the beginnings of most practical inventions, he will find that they had their origins in " pure science."

The great strides that have been made in recent years in research in the physical sciences have demonstrated more surely than had ever before been suspected, that science is a " homogeneous whole." No part of it then is without value in completing the entire picture. And if there be a homogeneity to the whole body of science, how much more true it is, that any single phase of it, such as meteorology, must possess a certain unity.

That wind circulation is a phenomenon of world-wide extent has long been known; there is a general surface circulation of the atmosphere from the polar regions toward the equator and a return back toward the poles at higher levels. The local disturbances in these major movements are of the first importance in understanding the causes of weather. But it is at once evident that such local phenomena cannot be fully appreciated until the fundamental or underlying causes behind them are more completely understood. When we consider that meteorologists have been forced to interpret and forecast weather from data drawn only from the middle and temperate latitudes, there is little cause for wonder that the results have not been more perfect. Science seeks in vain for an explanation, from known meteorological data, of the causes of such calamitous occurrences as the recent drought that left so much suffering in its wake in our own country. Is it not reasonable to suppose that if the answer is to be found in terrestrial causes, that the proper place now to seek further data is from the polar regions?

To quote Dr. Isaiah Bowman: "A calculation of the forces involved in a single localized low-pressure area prepare one to believe that the polar regions include centers of action of astounding size and of direct interest and practical importance to mankind in the temperate zones."

Even the most disinterested layman can well understand that such great permanent masses of ice as those which cover the Antarctic Continent and Greenland, with a total area greater than that of the United States and continental Canada combined and an estimated thickness of from two to ten thousand feet, must have a profound effect upon weather and even climate in more than a local sense. It has further been estimated that there is discharged from the polar regions into the warmer oceans every year, a volume of drift ice, so great that if it were evenly distributed over the land areas of the earth it would make a complete covering one foot in thickness! That such discharges are of major importance in the weather of parts of the southern hemisphere, at least, has long been known. For the volume of these seasonal outpourings of ice is not constant but shows considerable variation, and such great changes in weather have been coincident with such variations that there is little reason for not believing them to be related. Dr. Bowman [1] has pointed out that such correlations or relationships were noted long ago, and that between 1892 and 1897, Dr. Otto Petterson observed that there was " an enormous outburst of ice from the Antarctic which filled the Southern Ocean with ice floes and icebergs to such an extent that traffic between South America, Africa and Australia had to seek a more northerly route." Far-reaching climatic effects followed this discharge according to Dr. Petterson. Years of excessive rainfall were followed by excessive drought with consequent famine in India; the loss of cattle ran into the millions. Over a period of seven years over fifty million sheep valued at over $60,000,000 were lost in parts of Australia.

For him who wants an answer to that question What for? on purely practical grounds, surely here it is. I am not suggesting that complete meteorological data from the polar regions will enable man to forestall such emergencies as great droughts and the like, but we have good reason to suppose that they will enable him to predict with some assurance the times of their occurrence. Such data can only be gathered from many permanent stations. Professor Hobbs has been a pioneer in the establishment of such a station about the Greenland Ice Cap and Sir Hubert Wilkins' Antarctic explorations anticipate the establishment of such stations on that continent.

It is inevitable that scientific research in any new field should begin rather blindly; it has to feel its way to find its proper direction and it grows by accretion; it works by trial and error and naturally often finds itself running up blind alleys. Polar research has passed the blind alley stage. No expedition in these days could hope for support from

[1] Bowman, Isaiah. Polar Exploration, *Science*, Oct. 31, 1930, pp. 439–449.

any scientific bodies if it set out on a vague quest of knowledge and adventure. Little as we know about the Antarctic,
we yet know enough to realize that we can go looking for
specific things. I have pointed out how true and how practical this is from the standpoint of meteorology, and it
is likewise true that there are few fields in all science that
do not seek *new and specific light* on their particular problems from data that are available only in the polar regions.

Many manifestations of terrestrial magnetism, like meteorology, are still mysteries for lack of data which can come
only from the " ends of the earth." That further investigation of the earth's magnetic qualities has great practical
bearing upon the usefulness of the ordinary magnetic
compass is too evident to need amplification. To the radio
fan, magnetic storms, in so far as they affect his reception of
an evening's program, assume considerable importance;
the relationship of radio reception to the electrical conditions of the air is an almost unprospected field, especially
in polar latitudes. Hand in hand with such research goes
that associated with auroral observations and the relationship of all these phenomena to the recurrence of sun spots.
The Byrd Expedition was able, for the first time, to make
simultaneous observations on these interrelated phenomena, and correlations between them that are suggestive of
relationships of great interest and consequence were noted
and are fairly demanding further investigation.

Naturally in my own field of geological research I find
the most intriguing prospects in Antarctica. The greatest
problem in structural geology in all the world awaits solution here; namely is the Antarctic Continent one great
land mass or is it separated into two major parts by a
great trough-like connection between the Ross and Wed-

dell Seas? I do not believe the latter notion is any longer tenable, but definitive evidence is still lacking.

In the field of glaciation Antarctica offers opportunities of unparalleled interest for study. The scenery, the topography, in fact the physical geography in general, and therefore to a large extent the modes of life of the people of northern Europe and most of North America, owe their existence to the great ice sheets that submerged large parts of these continents during the Pleistocene or Ice Age, many thousands of years ago. We deduce the condition that must have existed then solely by inference; the origin of such distinctive features as the Great Lakes is still largely a mystery and estimates of the thickness of these great ice sheets vary from two to twenty thousand feet!

Since the Antarctic Continent is still virtually in the Ice Age and is covered with a great ice sheet comparable in all essential respects to those of Pleistocene time, it is a vast laboratory where we can, in a sense, actually observe the conditions that once obtained over such large areas of the northern continents. Instruments are now available which will make it possible and practicable for the next expedition that goes inland to measure the thickness of the ice. This will reveal the contour of the underlying lands and by comparison will give us definitive information about the thickness of the Pleistocene ice sheets.

Great stories about the past climates and life of the Antarctic are still waiting to be read in the rocks. Nowhere in the world is the hunt for fossils filled with prospects of greater promise. From fossils we shall learn whether the present isolation of the Antarctic continent is a recent condition, or whether it has enjoyed such isolation throughout much of recorded geological time. It is in the study of extinct life that we must seek the solution of one of the greatest problems in animal migration.

There are such remarkable affinities between certain fauna (particularly marsupials [2]) of South America and Australia that many zoölogists and paleontologists believe they can only be explained on the basis of a former land connection between Antarctica on the one hand and South America and Australia on the other. If the present isolation of the continent has been a characteristic feature for long periods of geological time, then these remarkable faunal affinities will have to find explanation in some other way — as for instance the result of migrations from more extensive lands to the north. In any event, as Dr. Robert Cushman Murphy [3] has pointed out, definitive light or proof "would be forthcoming only through the discovery of marsupials or other pertinent materials in fossiliferous beds of Antarctica."

Finally it is probably the great challenge that it offers to geographical research, due to its isolation and inaccessibility, that makes the Antarctic so alluring to the explorer. This challenge is more apparent if we briefly contrast the two polar regions. Within the parallel of 60 degrees north latitude there live more than 1,000,000 people many of whom thrive on such industries as mining, fishing, and lumbering; indeed some of the greatest timber tracts in all the world lie within these northern latitudes.

About the South Pole is the highest, the coldest, and the most forbidding of all the continents and within the whole

[2] Animals with pouches on lower part of abdomen of females in which the young, born comparatively undeveloped, are carried. The present-day kangaroo of Australia is an example.

[3] Murphy, Robert Cushman. Problems of Polar Research, Am. Geog. Soc., 1928, p. 358.

range of the corresponding latitudes indicated for the north, there are but a scant few primitive forms of plant life, no land animals larger than an insect, no trees, and not one human habitant!

Every other continent can be reached by crossing less then 100 miles of shallow seas, whereas the Antarctic is separated on every side from the nearest continental land mass by not less than 600 miles of oceanic waters. Much of the coastline remains to be, even roughly, charted, and only within the narrow limits of the Ross Sea Sector has the continent been penetrated to any great depth. The continent as a whole is still largely unexplored as may be seen from the insert in the map opposite page 124. It is still the terra incognita of all the world; in fact if all the other unexplored areas were added together the total would be less than the unknown regions in this vast continent.

To predict the benefits that will come to man from such further Antarctic research as that suggested above is not within the scope of this book, and to make the merest suggestion as to the ultimate usefulness of this continent on the basis of its natural resources would be the sheerest kind of guess work. That it contains enormous coal reserves we know, and that it may contain undreamed mineral wealth is within reason — but we don't know. I do not like to enlist support for Antarctic exploration on the basis of its practical consequences. There is a far deeper and more fundamental reason for it than the ultimate motive of exploitation.

It does not matter from what angle or relationship to existing knowledge in other parts of the world we may approach the Antarctic, whether it be the role it played in the evolution of the earth in past geological times, or whether it be its present important role in the meteor-

ological set up of the world — we always come up against
the same question — we don't know — we don't know.
And is not this after all the most vital reason why Antarctic exploration must go on? Is not the very primal
and fundamental urge that makes man want to know just
for the sake of knowing a more real reason for it all than
any thought of practical benefit? It is, after all, the lure of
the unknown and the restless spirit of mankind will never
stop until every bit of it has been explored. It is man's
never-to-be-satisfied thirst for knowledge. It is bigger than
peoples or congresses or parliaments and though a lethargy
of public and private interest may from time to time slow
it up, nothing can stop it, so long as man is man.

We have been in these late days genuinely touched by
the picture of Michaelson's devotion to the work that has
inspired his whole life. I suppose one of the most vital
aspects of science is, that in its lure, a few souls may find
that selfless detachment from life that makes the contribution of the individual himself, vastly more important
than the results of his research. Polar exploration has been
called the "physical expression of the intellectual pas-
sion," and in its history there have been many Michael-
sons. Nansen was one and Scott was another. One can
search the history of physical and biological research in
vain for any more complete devotion to the quest for truth
than that which inspired Scott and his men, after the dire-
ness of their position must have been apparent, to carry
on with a bag of rock specimens which was found in a
cairn within a few miles of their last resting place. But
it was a bag of specimens which as Cherry-Gerard phrases
it "dated a continent and may elucidate the whole history
of plant life."

So long as things written are preserved will the story

of these men and their heroic end stir the imagination of man and thrill the heart of the school boy. Why? Because they created an ideal that will shine for all time to lift men above the gray monotony of everyday life.

But Scott did not leave England and home to create one of the world's tragedies. Nor would he have done so had the sole purpose of his expedition been the attainment of the South Pole. I believe that with his men and equipment he would have reached the Pole and returned in safety to McMurdo Sound had he attempted to do nothing else. But Scott was sincerely interested in gathering knowledge about the Antarctic and had brought together a very comprehensive group of scientists, with the result that his program of field operations became a diversified one and it sapped strength from the polar trek. It had been necessary for him to angle for support for his expedition on the basis of the achievement of the Pole as the main object. It was never the sole object in his mind.

Likewise I have little doubt but that had Admiral Byrd sought support for such an extensive expedition as he had planned, solely on the basis of the research that he hoped the expedition to accomplish, he would have failed. And had he failed in his polar flight the larger scientific results of the expedition would have been viewed in a much less generous light by the general public.

The North and South Poles do not represent the most inaccessible parts of either of the polar regions and furthermore just to reach these exact mathematical points has never been, in itself, an achievement of the first importance. It is the knowledge of what lies about the poles that is of value, yet popular fancy has surrounded the poles themselves with such a glamour that any expedition that has not included in its purposes the reaching of a Pole by some method or other, has lost much standing with the public. And since the public, and not government nor scientific institutions, has contributed most to the financing of such expeditions, it has been necessary to cater to this popular fancy.

Had Wilkins' flight from Alaska to Spitsbergen been via the North Pole, his achievement would have been much more highly acclaimed by the public. Yet it was the greatest flight that has yet been made in the Arctic and netted much more knowledge than a flight across the Pole would have done.

But may we not hope that the day is past when we must seek support for polar research in terms of spectacular and heroic effort, must we still hold up the challenge that nowhere has knowledge been purchased at such great cost? The polar regions are as definite fields for specific research as a laboratory and I hope that the next expedition that asks for public and private support to go north or south, with a proper program for research, will not have to hold up the lure of knowledge that is " baited by suffering and death " to get proper support.

So much knowledge is now available to us from the experience of those who have pioneered the way that polar exploration should become increasingly easy and less dangerous. After all there is no virtue whatever in doing things the hardest way, and come what may, no matter how we attack it, the Antarctic will certainly for many years to come present sufficient obstacles to challenge the most virile. I cannot conceive of the time ever coming when it will be easy to carry on detailed field studies there.

For him who must climb the glaciers and scale the mountains there will always be the dangers from crevasses and avalanches. To anticipate all such natural hazards is not within the province of any man. But we can hopefully expect that there will be no more Captain Oates and no more Scotts. Only thus will we be worthy of their sacrifices.

And now I come to the end of this rather diffuse chapter and the end of the book with the realization that Dr. Finley has suggested the simplest and therefore perhaps the most adequate answer to the question Why?, when he tells of the ambitions of the English schoolmaster Leigh-Mallory. This Englishman had once attempted to climb Mt. Everest and had failed and was back in England making preparations for a second attempt, an attempt on which he lost his life, and when asked why he left his friends and the comfort of all that he had at home just to try to reach the summit of this, the highest mountain in the world, replied:

" Because it is there."

And because the Antarctic is there, I want to go back. I want to find out where the Queen Maud Mountains end; I want to know more about the recorded writing on the rock pages of Antarctic geological history — more about its past climates and the life that has thrived in this now " lifeless continent " — more about the ancestors of that fascinating and restless little bundle of curiosity, the Adélie penguin and his great cousin the Emperor. And I had rather go back to the Antarctic and find a fossil marsupial than three gold mines!

INDEX